The Ripples

from

Our Stones

The Ripples

from

Our Stones

Redeeming Inmate
11699-077

STEPHEN D. GRIFFITTS

Cover Photos: Stefan Milivojevic (iStock photo #1446030884)
Cover Design: Patrice N. Griffitts

ASIN: B0CVNLBX7D
ISBN: 9798878807555
Imprint: Independently Published

First Edition, February 8, 2024

Dedication

For Brother-Man

THANK YOU FOR SHARING your astonishing story with me. I am honored to assist you in dealing with your most dreaded task – personally examining and publicly confessing those things about your past of which you are not proud. I know that doing so makes you exceedingly uncomfortable, as it would anyone. I encourage you to remember your own words.

> *"I want to glorify God, but I am afraid*
> *that I will have to publicly confess*
> *the ugly truth about myself,*
> *things of which I am not proud,*
> *and that make me very uncomfortable.*
> *But I know I must ultimately do His will*
> *at some point if He is to be glorified.*
> *And so, I am sure I shall."*

God promised His will in 1 John 1:9 (NIV), which says, "If we confess our sins, He is faithful and just and will forgive us our sins and purify us of all unrighteousness."

—— **Little Brother**

Epigraph

The Ripple Effect

(Noun) – A spreading, pervasive, and usually unintentional effect or influence.

—— **Miriam-Webster Dictionary**

*"Just as ripples spread out
when a single pebble is dropped into water,
the actions of individuals
can have far reaching effects."*

—— **Dalai Lama**

Contents

Preface

JayBFree

IN NOVEMBER 2015, my then-fiancé Patrice and I traveled to Pottsboro, Texas, to the home of my friend Jay Emerson. By then, Jay had established himself as a respected professional restorer of antique and classic wooden boats. We went there to interview him for an article I was writing for *The Brass Bell*, the quarterly print magazine of The Chris-Craft Antique Boat Club.

I had met Jay several years earlier at a meeting of the Wooden Boat Association of North Texas. My initial impression of Jay was that he was a friendly, gregarious, big-hearted, and fun-loving bear of a man. To an introvert like me, Jay's personality was bigger than life. His incessant loud talking and constant laughter could be overwhelming sometimes, but his warmth and sincerity were undeniably endearing. While Jay enjoyed being the center of attention, if you were in his presence, he always made you feel like *you* were the center of his attention.

Had I not already known about Jay's personal history, I would never have believed the tale he would share on that crisp fall day. The three of us sat in lawn chairs in his backyard around a fire pit burning a lively fire. I mounted my video camera on a tripod, aimed it at Jay, and turned it on to record.

Dressed in a plaid flannel shirt, camouflage trousers, and ankle-high combat-style boots, Jay sat cross-legged as he leafed through a copy of *The Brass Bell* I had given him. I had prepared a five-page outline of what I wanted him to discuss during the interview. He listened attentively as I laid out my plan. Finally, when I had explained the entire outline, I said, "This is what I had in mind, but if you have a general idea of what I'm looking for, how about if you just start talking and tell me your story as you see it?"

It was as if I had lit a bottle rocket. Jay started talking, and as I filmed him, in his inimitable animated manner, he alternately talked, shouted, whispered, laughed, and wept for almost five hours as he recounted some of his story's more significant and poignant events. In later visits and phone conversations, some of Jay's so-called 'Partners in Crime' would also discuss their respective roles and perspectives on the story.

By the time Jay finally talked himself out, my brain was overflowing. Patrice's head and mine were both spinning from sensory overload. I had finished my cigar, and Patrice and I had downed several glasses of wine while listening to Jay. I had brought a cigar for him, which he never lit, being too busy talking. He also milked a single glass of wine for several hours and still left most of it in the glass.

I realized the material I collected from this interview would not be suitable for a family-oriented boating magazine article. Nevertheless, that day, Patrice and I heard the most profound, compelling, and deeply disturbing but honest and transparent story of a shameless life of crime and consequential imprisonment, resulting in unimaginable suffering and inevitable unbearable despair.

Today, all who know Jay think of him as the man who greets everyone with an infectious, full-faced grin accompanied by a booming belly laugh and a mighty bear hug that lasts for a long time. All acknowledge him as a man who considers it his primary mission to make everyone around him feel welcome and comfortable, who subordinates his needs to those of others, and who is genuinely respected and loved by his fellow man.

Over time, I came to regard Jay as one of the finest gentlemen I have ever known. While I am fully aware of his criminal background, I see him through the filter of the Lord Jesus Christ, who has washed him in His blood. Despite his past behaviors, thanks to his belief in God, Jay's soul is now as clean and white as a sheet.

So, in early 2016, I asked Jay to serve as the Best Man for my marriage to Patrice. I couldn't think of anyone else I would rather have do the job. He honored me by graciously accepting my request.

On September 17, 2016, the day of our wedding, Jay and his wife, PJ, made the two-hundred-mile drive to our house in North Richland Hills, Texas, from McAlester, Oklahoma.

Upon their arrival, Jay limped into the house and explained that he had crashed his hang glider earlier in the week and was in a great deal of pain. He needed to lie down for a few minutes to rest his back, so I led him to my office down the hall. Jay cautiously shuffled over to the space between my desk and the wall, where he laid himself supine on the floor. He crossed his hands over his chest, looked up at Kasey, our turquoise-haired wedding planner, and said, "Darlin', would you please bring me three Aspirin and two shots of the finest scotch you can find?" Unfortunately, we had neither Aspirin nor scotch, so I sent Kasey back with three Tylenol and two shots of Jack Daniels instead.

We held the wedding at our house, and by the time the ceremony rolled around, Jay was up and at 'em and rarin' to go!

When it was time, he put his jacket on, slapped me on the back, and laughed uproariously. "Come on, Little Brother, Let's get this show on the road!" he shouted. "We've got places to go and people to meet!"

And so, we did.

I call my special friend 'Brother-Man,' and he calls me 'Little Brother.' I value that highly. It is an expression of brotherly love from a man I appreciate and respect.

—— **Stephen D. Griffitts**
Author

Acknowledgments

I WISH TO EXPRESS my most sincere appreciation to all those who contributed to the creation of *The Ripples from Our Stones: Redeeming Inmate 11699-077.*

This story's central character and focus, Jay Emerson, provided the core material for developing the main storyline during my five-hour taped interview of him at his home in Pottsboro, Texas, in 2015. Jay's inimitable demonstrative and emotional storytelling style contributed to the main message's flavor and flair. Seven years after that initial interview, he encouraged and motivated me to find and review those video tapes and create this book.

Since then, Jay scoured his personal files and brought me letters, photos, newspaper clippings, and other materials to help flesh out the story. He also answered a seemingly infinite number of questions needed to clarify my understanding of the people, places, and events during his visits to my home and various phone conversations.

Jay also made available to me the unique insights of his wonderful wife, Paula Jean (PJ) Goodner, who was trained in counseling psychology at Southeastern Oklahoma State University and has known Jay for more than twenty years. Accordingly, she provided some intimate insights into Jay's psyche and history, which extended the breadth and depth of the story and, frankly, forced the exposure of some of the aspects of Jay's life that were more painful for him to face.

Jay also facilitated access to some of his so-called "Partners-in-Crime," each of whom had a greater or lesser involvement in the various criminal activities in which Jay participated. Some of these people Jay brought to my house so we could have a face-to-face conversation, and others spoke with me on the phone. I recorded all these conversations so as not to lose any details and then had them professionally transcribed. I weaved their statements about their activities throughout the book as appropriate. These contributors included Messrs. Gary Athans, Bill Dippo, Randy Hauch, Gary House, Dana McChesnee, David Nichols, and Van Warren. Thanks to all of you gentlemen, for your willingness to speak with me and the valuable insights you provided.

I also wish to thank the members of the Whyte Dove Writing Group in Quitman, Texas, for their helpful insights into various story components. We authors write things and then read them how we intended for them to be read. However, others may not see it that way, so it's helpful to have input from third parties, both experienced authors and prolific readers. What is essential is not what we intended for the readers to see but rather what images, thoughts, feelings, and understandings our words provoke in the minds of our readers based on the words we have written. The two are not always the same. Accomplishing that reconciliation is a challenge for any writer.

Of course, my greatest supporter and my harshest critic has been my lovely wife, Patrice Griffitts. As I finished drafts of each chapter, I asked Patrice to read them and give me her honest impressions. Over time, we came to a mutual understanding that 'sugar-coated, tell me what you think I want you to say' critiques have no value to me. They are, in fact, quite irritating and a waste of time. But whenever she gives me one of those, I know that what I have written is shit. And when I acknowledge that, she tells me the truth. As painful as that can be, after I quit pouting and take the time to think through what she had said, I find that her comments are always meaningful, so I make the appropriate changes to my text, which invariably represent the majority of her comments. And the story is always better as a result.

My favorite comment came after Patrice read an early draft of, "Prelude – Rooster," which I subsequently removed from the book. She read this story, of which I was quite proud, then said, "Frankly, Steve, this sucks. It is entirely too polite. Guys in prison don't talk like this. You need to add some profanity for this to be believable." This from my 'good Catholic girl' wife. However, I realized she was right, and made the adjustments, which changed the book's whole personality.

However, this change probably pretty much wiped out my chances of marketing the book as Christian material, which it really is. Nevertheless, I thought about it and said, "You know, you're right. These guys are coarse men. They're convicts in prison. They don't say, 'Please' and 'Thank you.' They're more likely to say something like, "What the f***k you lookin' at, m**********r?"

Patrice also designed and created the beautiful cover for this book.

So, thank you, love, for being brutally honest. I really appreciate it. Truthfully, I do. And I love you all the more for it.

At the beginning of my acknowledgments, I said, "The central character and the focus of this story was Jay Emerson." Well, that is not entirely true. Jay was only the vehicle through which the Lord Jesus Christ accomplished His objectives. Jay needed salvation, and Jesus pushed Jay's face into the mud long enough for him to realize that. Jay needed to change his ways, and Jesus showed him the path to accomplish that. Jay needed redemption and healing, and Jesus showed him what he had to do to get that. All Jay had to do was follow His lead, as painful and uncomfortable as that might be.

There is a verse in the Bible, II Corinthians 5:17 (NIV), that personifies the story of Jay Emerson. "Therefore, if anyone is in Christ, he is a new creation; the old has gone, the new has come!"

— **Stephen D. Griffitts**
Author and Your Brother in Christ

Forward

The Man I Know and Love

*"You were taught, with regard to your former way of life,
to put off your old self,
which is being corrupted by its deceitful desires;
to be made new in the attitude of your minds;
and to put on the new self,
created to be like God in true righteousness and holiness."*

—— **Ephesians 4:22-24 (NIV)**

I AM PAULA JEAN GOODNER, also known as 'PJ.' I have been the wife of Jay Caldwell Emerson for nineteen years and knew him for two more years before that. I love and adore Jay and believe in him implicitly. He is a good man with a good heart, making him well worth the effort. And, mind you, the effort is significant.

My experience as a Licensed Professional Counselor Supervisor has given me a unique ability to better understand Jay's mind, heart, behaviors, and the reasoning behind those behaviors.

Jay is a very complicated man, and I will admit that living with him requires a great deal of patience.

This man has experienced a tough life. In his youth, he endured the many dysfunctional behaviors of his family of origin, being kidnapped and moved to Canada by his mother, and then being relocated halfway across the United States in the middle of his high school years by his father. These things left Jay confused, disoriented, and headed down a bad road.

As an adult, he submitted to the manipulative, domineering, selfish, and unhealthy influence of his Cousin Buck Cameron, five years his elder. This influence soon led both men to creating a drug smuggling ring. Ultimately, after living lives of crime for more than twenty years, they each accumulated three felony drug convictions. Consequently, the judicial system regarded them both as 'career criminals,' earning a life without parole sentence for Buck and a twenty-five-year sentence for Jay in federal prison.

Jay spent approximately fourteen of the years between the ages of thirty and forty-eight, incarcerated in a series of county jails and state and federal penal facilities, leaving him an 'institutionalized' man. He became institutionalized by developing beliefs and practices that were established as a common and accepted part of the prison system and culture. However, many of these beliefs and practices were incongruent and incompatible with life in the 'outside' world.

So, all those years that the rest of us were learning how to survive in the outside world and get along in society, Jay lived among a community of people with the mentality and social skills of fourteen- or fifteen-year-olds. This was the general social structure for prison inmates.

As you might expect, this experience profoundly affected the man he would become.

Once he was released from prison, life became more complicated for Jay. He had not developed social skills and common behaviors that would work in the outside world. He had learned how to live in prison, but not outside of prison.

My relationship with Jay began soon after his release from prison. As you might expect, this experience has not been without its challenges. But the walk through it has been a learning and growing experience for both of us, and I'm glad we made it to the other side of the worst part.

I love that Jay has come such a long way. It is an ongoing process, but his willingness and hard work continue to transform him daily, and he is sincerely trying to do better.

But it is exhausting, putting it mildly, because he has so many needs and carryovers.

As his wife, I can tell you that Jay is very insecure. I firmly believe, as he does, that had I not come along all those years ago, he probably would be living in a bus or something, he would be using, and he would not be where he is today.

As of this writing, Jay is seventy-one years old. His health has been in decline of late, and his insecurities have become more advanced. He requires a tremendous amount of personal attention. He takes things personally and sincerely needs everyone to like him.

Sometimes, Jay leaves me little love notes here and there. I had a terrible cold recently. While I was sick, he did all the cooking and most of the cleanup in the kitchen. And he would say, "What can I do to help you today?"

Other times, he will get upset about something and then vent about it. But I never say a word in response until later when he is calm and ready to listen. I find it best to wait until people are calm because you cannot work out problems when they are still upset and argumentative.

<<<>>>

Jay often asks me, "What can I do to help?"

What I really want to say in response, and I often do say, is, "If you want to help, get out there in your boat shop and do some work."

But I try to be gentler than that because you get more flies with honey than with vinegar. Right?

Jay had never learned proper work discipline at a straight job. During his years in prison, he worked less than a half-day at a time and took naps. He grew up with that, which is still his work practice today.

His work practices are a sensitive issue with me because I'm just the opposite. I typically put in almost eighty hours over a six-and-a-half-day work week.

While opposites often attract, I sometimes think God has a warped sense of humor about that. But I love him because he is a good person and always strives to be better.

My husband would like me to be with him in all times of strife. Sometimes, that can be smothering for me, but I understand that there are a lot of carryovers from his childhood and time in prison. So, I try to accommodate him the best I can.

<<<>>>

Jay is self-employed as a professional restorer of antique and classic wooden boats. When he is restoring a boat for a customer, he frequently does way more work than his customer expected, but he wants them to like him, so he tries to please them by not billing the total amount. He perpetually gives them this and that for free, and consequently, he doesn't make any money.

He is a magnificent artist in his woodworking. His product is beautiful and his boats have won many awards at boat shows around the country. Other people call on him for advice on how to do things on their boats. He even will travel to help others at his own expense. Most of his customers are very well off financially and would probably pay him for the time if they knew how much he invested in their precious treasures.

Jay is forever promising things to people. But every day, he wakes up and decides what he will work on that day. This is without regard to his previous commitments. So, I often have to remind him to complete his promised tasks first.

My husband is a sincere caregiver. When I had an accident, he couldn't have been more caring. My mother lived to be one hundred and three years old. As she was in decline, Jay got up at night with me to help care for her. And when my sister had a serious accident, he was there to assist in any way we needed.

Jay claims that he is a man without compassion, but I don't believe that. I see a man with great compassion. He steps up to the plate when there is a need. He is a natural caregiver.

When first becoming a Christian, he was absorbed in wanting to become a man of God, a man of value, and a good husband.

He is a child of God, and he seeks the Lord. His family of origin, prison, and drugs have left terrible scars. He is still learning to accept grace and release his guilt and shame.

He and I begin each day with Bible study and prayer together. We read a devotional, read the Bible, and pray together each morning.

When he moved to Washington to attend boatbuilding school, I saw no signs of Christianity in him. While he was a believer, he did not go to church. I did not see any practice of his faith. He would applaud me for going on mission trips and be supportive of that. But that was before we got married.

The 'Walk to Emmaus' program was a significant influence on Jay. The best way I can describe it is that it's about being immersed in God's love and is very affirming. The program was of enormous benefit in moving Jay's faith journey forward.

Then he earned his way to being on the lay teaching teams and gradually became a lay director. Being with those men in that atmosphere was a big thing for him. It was very holy and meaningful, which has helped his spiritual walk, too. Part of that was because it made him feel important to give talks and work his way up, but also, it was another time of spiritual growth.

This book has been in the making for over a year and a half. Because of Jay's contribution to that effort, his transformation in that time has been phenomenal. Nevertheless, having this book written about him has sometimes been quite arduous for Jay. He has had to look deep down inside himself to examine who he is, where he came from, his life choices, the consequences of those life choices, and his willingness to change himself. Then he had to make a public confession about those things. Having this book written has been an excellent vehicle for helping him do that.

Jay has grown quite a bit while working with the author on this book. Now, he seeks to try to please, and he aims to try to be a better person than he has ever been. Looking inward has been an eye-opening experience for him, if not a painful catharsis.

I would say that today, Jay is striving very hard to be more of the person he wants to be and is more aware of who that person is.

Does he have slip-ups? Yes, of course. But he is really trying to be a man of God, a man of faith. He wants to be a good example. He wants to be used by God.

Jay has a very kind, sweet side. But it's like living with a child that wants to do right. He wants to please his mama, which is me, without having all the requisite skills. Is he learning? Yes, indeed. Has he changed a lot? Oh, you bet'cha. But it has been a prolonged process with him. He works on it every day. He is very aware of what he wants, and he wants it desperately.

I will confess, if Jay were not trying so hard, if he were not such a good man at heart, and if I had not made a promise in front of God, I could not stay in this relationship because it is just too exhausting.

But, in the meantime, I will continue to love and adore Jay and believe in him implicitly.

I love you, Jay Caldwell Emerson. I pray God's blessings on you.

—— **Paula Jean Goodner (aka "PJ")**

Pardon My French, S'il Vous Plaît

*"Let us swear while we may,
for in Heaven, it will not be allowed."*

—— **Mark Twain**

The Ripples from Our Stones is a story of convicts, hardened criminals serving time in Federal prisons. They are not the most gentlemanly, mannerly, or delicate men; indeed, they are not the politest. Mostly, they are downright rough, crude, and coarse men. As such, they are prolific users of foul language, routinely using the 'F-word' at least once in every sentence.

It is the way they are and the way of life where they live. It is the common language of their community, their 'power language.' To be otherwise, might make them appear weak.

Therefore, I caution you to be prepared to read some words your mother long ago forbade you to use.

It is not my desire or preference to write this way, but I feel I should be as realistic as possible in the dialogue and sometimes the general discussion. The profusion of profanity is only an attempt at authenticity. It is not central to the message.

Please do not be distracted by the foul language, and instead focus on the more profound, more spiritual message that requires you to read all the way to the end.

Thank you for your understanding and accommodation. My apologies if I offend you.

—— **Stephen D. Griffitts**
Author

Act One

CRIMINAL ASPIRATIONS

The Cannabis Leaf [1]

THE LEAF OF THE CANNABIS PLANT is probably the most recognized symbol of the marijuana plant and the cannabis culture. The leaves come in a variety of shapes and sizes. Most have five or seven points (blades), but some can have nine. Typically, indica plants have short, fat leaves, and sativa plants have long, skinny leaves. Leaves are essential for the growing cannabis plant. They act like solar panels, absorbing light for the plant, and are necessary for photosynthesis.

CHAPTER ONE

And the Chain Goes On and On and On

"Choices are like stones cast into the waters of life, creating ripples that extend far beyond what we can see."

—— **Dr. Lucas D. Shallua**

THE SETTING SUN shimmered silently through the trees across the water. I stood barefoot at water's edge tossing smooth black stones into the lake. As each stone hit the still water, concentric circles radiated far away from the point of entrance. The expanding circles seemed to spread endlessly. With my stones I had disrupted this perfectly serene scene yet knew not the ultimate impact of my actions. Small actions can lead to more significant changes, even if we can't see how far they can reach. When one thing occurs, it has an impact on other situations, and the chain goes on and on and on.

This is the 'Ripple Effect.'

The 'Stones' are the actions we take to cause those ripples.

My name is Jay Caldwell Emerson, and I have touched many people's lives, and not necessarily in a good way. Perhaps many of those people would have lived normal lives and gone on to become productive members of society were it not for my actions. How I lived and the path I chose to follow changed people's lives, resulting in some going to prison and others dying. The drugs I sold – marijuana, cocaine, crack cocaine, methamphetamines, and heroin – all damaged lives, destroyed relationships, and caused death,

2

whether by overdose, accident, or even murder. And those drugs certainly created great heartache. Nearly everyone I worked with ended up going to prison, and many did serious time, destroying their futures and their family relationships.

God corroborated this idea of the consequences of our actions having an effect far beyond our realization when, in Exodus 20:5-6 (NIV), He said, *"...for I, the Lord your God, am a jealous God, punishing the children for the sin of the fathers to the third and fourth generation of those who hate me, but showing love to a thousand generations of those who love me and keep my commandments."*

I became involved with marijuana when I was a young and foolish teenager. I did not realize it would drive my destiny, becoming my life-long passion, my career's focus, and the path to the destruction of my life and those of others.

Rather, I thought of it as a simple matter of dollars and cents. I have always been a numbers guy, so if you figure moving sixteen ounces of weed will make a certain amount of profit, what's gonna happen when you do ten pounds? And, of course, your mind starts working the numbers. You start thinking, wow, this is the way to go. This is gonna make me some big money. This is gonna open up doors and avenues that I've never had available to me in any way, shape, or form.

So, I saw the marijuana smuggling business as a unique opportunity for me to become a powerful kingpin. I would be influential among certain crowds, from lining out cocaine on the tables at nightclubs to doing big deals and being the 'Man.' When I walked into a club, everybody would know me.

That's what I thought I wanted to do. So, from the age of seventeen, I eventually got all my friends working with me in supplying and developing distribution channels for all the marijuana lids I could make from a kilo brick. By the time I was twenty-two, we had developed a fourteen-man import-export and distribution network.

Of course, at that young and presumably invincible age, we never gave any thought to the fact that this was a highly illegal activity that could end with us being arrested and sent to prison.

Nah, don't worry about that. We're professionals (i.e., teenagers.) We know what we're doing. Besides, nothing bad is ever gonna happen to us. Right? Bad things only happen to other people.

These were '*our stones.*'

The *'ripples'* reached far beyond.

CHAPTER TWO

The Sulphur Springs Clique

"There may be no secrets in small towns,
but there are no strangers either.

—— R.A. Mathis

BUCK CAMERON AND JAY EMERSON were first cousins and members of two closely-knit families. Siblings Richard Henry Cameron, father of Buck Cameron, and Diane Cameron Emerson, mother of Jay Emerson, linked the two clans. Both groups were embedded in an informal social structure referred to as 'The Sulphur Springs Clique.' Allegedly, the members of this group privately condoned, if not openly encouraged, certain inappropriate social behaviors.

It may well have been that hereditary influences combined with environmental commonalities contributed to these two men following similar paths in life. However, their disparate responses and choices of direction made all the difference in their respective outcomes.

The history of the two families originated in the little town of Sulphur Springs. The Hopkins County Seat was eighty miles east of Dallas on Interstate 30 in East Texas. Founded as 'Bright Star' in the late 1840s, pioneers built homes near the more than one hundred natural springs bubbling from the land.

In 1871, the townspeople appropriately renamed the town 'Sulphur Springs.' They marketed the area as a health resort due to the healing waters flowing beneath the surface of the East Texas soil. The following year, the railroad extended its line to Mineola.

5

Visitors and settlers came in great numbers to benefit from the mineral springs and sulfur baths they had heard about.

In 1937, the Carnation Milk Company opened a processing plant in Sulphur Springs, which paved the way for large-scale dairy farming throughout the area. Hopkins County played home to more than six hundred grade-A dairies. The county earned the official 'Dairy Capital of Texas' title in the Fifties and retained it until 1990.

The town had a predominately white population of around nine thousand in the Seventies and Eighties when most of this story took place. The local dairy industry supported the economy, and watching the Wildcats play high school football was the chief source of entertainment. Otherwise, Sulphur Springs was a nondescript, small East Texas town with generally traditional Southern values.

Though the area's young adults called the town 'Suffer Springs' or sometimes 'Sofa Springs,' it was referred to by the city fathers as 'Celebration City.' In the Downtown District, Celebration Plaza featured locally grown produce, homemade arts and crafts, entertainment, and more.

This was the home of Buck and Jay and their families.

Exhibit 1 – The Cameron Family

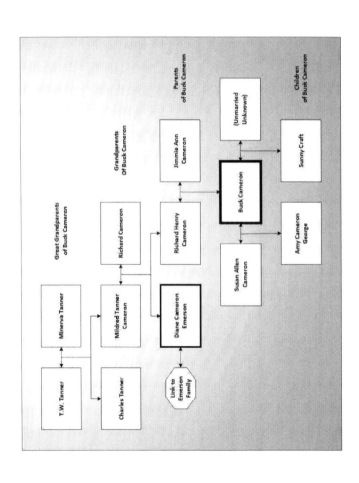

CHAPTER THREE

The Camerons

"Alcohol is the reduced form of spirit.
Therefore, many people, lacking spirit, take to drink.
They fill themselves with alcohol."

—— **Carl Jung**

T.W. TANNER founded the Tanner Furniture and Funeral Home, the primary funeral service provider in Sulphur Springs. The furniture company built wooden coffins for the community in the late nineteenth and early twentieth centuries. In 1901, the funeral home became its own business.

T.W. and his wife, Minerva Tanner, had two children, Charles and Mildred Tanner. Charles Tanner was said to be a mean old sonovabitch who hated everybody, and they hated him in return. He wanted nothing to do with the family business. Mildred Tanner married Richard Cameron, and when T.W. died and Minerva grew too old to manage the company, Richard took over as the company's sole manager.

Mildred and Richard bore a son, Richard Henry Cameron, in 1930. When Richard Henry was sixteen, he started college at North Texas State University in Denton, about one hundred fifteen miles west of Sulphur Springs. At such an early age, Richard Henry's mind was still very impressionable, and he did not have the maturity or judgment of a young adult necessary to operate successfully in that environment. Consequently, Richard Henry took up drinking while in college and remained a rabid alcoholic all his life.

As wealthy and affluent as the Cameron family was, for the most part, they were nearly all alcoholics.

Richard Henry married Jimmie Ann Cameron and they bore a son, Buck Cameron, in 1948. By the time the son was born, the Cameron family owned and operated the Tanner Furniture and Funeral Home. The business had become quite successful, making the family somewhat wealthy. This wealth allowed Buck to lead a charmed and spoiled life.

Charmed, that is, except for a drunk driver killing his mother, Jimmy Ann, when Buck was only three, and his father, Richard Henry, dying from alcoholism at forty-five, when Buck was twenty-six.

Exhibit 2 – The Emerson Family

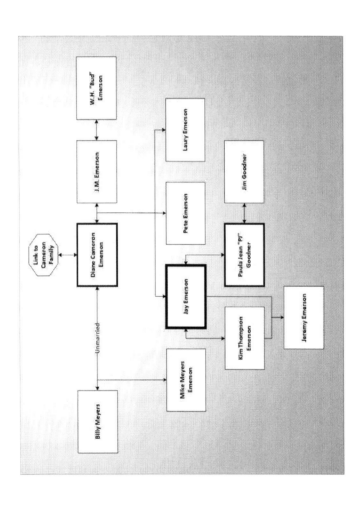

CHAPTER FOUR

The Emersons

"I loved my mother, even despite her faults.
She was my mother, after all.
That had to count for something. Right?"

—— Jay Emerson

MILDRED TANNER CAMERON and Richard Cameron also bore a daughter, Diane Cameron. The young girl became pregnant at fourteen by an American Indian of the Cherokee Nation named Billy Meyers, who hailed from Sulphur Springs. She delivered a son, Mike Meyers, at fifteen in June 1948.

Diane later married J.M. Emerson, a basic and down-to-earth man. When J.M. was just a baby, his father died in an oil rig accident resulting from a lightning strike. After that, his older brothers raised him.

After the marriage, J.M. adopted Mike and gave him the Emerson surname. Mike Meyers Emerson visited his birth father, Billy Meyers, from time to time but never had much of a relationship with him until his later years in college.

Jay Emerson became the first-born son of J.M. and Diane Cameron Emerson in February 1953.

The Emerson family moved to Sulphur Springs, where they lived for Jay's first and second years of elementary school.

J.M. and Diane Emerson divorced in 1959 when Jay was six years old. Remarrying each other two years later, the family moved to Thousand Oaks, forty miles northwest of downtown Los Angeles, on Highway 101 in Southern California. There, he started school in the third grade.

Besides the older half-brother, Mike, Jay had another brother, Pete Emerson, who was four years younger. Pete died in a motorcycle accident when he was only nineteen or twenty. Jay also had a sister, Laury Emerson, who came along thirteen years after Jay.

Mike returned to Sulfur Springs after graduating from Thousand Oaks High School in 1967 and began college twenty miles west at East Texas State University. While in college, Mike worked as a delivery boy for the family business, Tanner Furniture and Funeral Home.

"I always thought of ours as a loving, middle-class family," Jay says, "I never felt neglected or in need of anything. And I loved my mother, even despite her faults. She was my mother, after all. That had to count for something. Right?"

CHAPTER FIVE

A Less than Stellar Student

*"He's like a pinball wildly bouncing
off everything and everyone in the room."*

— **Gladys Allen**

ONE AFTERNOON after school in 1959, the clack-clack-clack of Diane Emerson's kitten heel pumps rang out as she hurried down the hallway of Austin Elementary School. She was searching for Room Twenty-Four, where Jay's first-grade teacher, Miss Gladys Allen, awaited her for their scheduled parent-teacher conference.

"Miss Allen?" Diane said, peeking her head into the room's doorway.

"Yes."

"I'm Diane Emerson. Jay's mother."

"Oh, yes! Come in. You're right on time," Miss Allen said. "Please, sit down," she motioned toward several child-sized plastic and steel chairs.

"Thank you," Diane said as she hung her purse strap over the seatback and sat in the tiny chair. "Hmm… I feel like a giant in this chair." She smiled slightly as she commented. *Jeez, this girl can't even be out of high school yet.*

The pert, twenty-something teacher smiled back and sat in another small chair facing Diane. Prim and proper, she was conservatively dressed in a black business suit, expensive-looking shoes, and carefully manicured fingernails. Brushing her long brunette hair back with one hand, she pulled a student report card from the basket beneath her chair.

"Misses Emerson, thank you for coming in this afternoon. I would like to speak with you about your son's progress this year."

"Oh, okay, sure," Diane said nervously, trying to conceal her dread about this conversation.

Looking around the room, Diane noticed the young teacher's college diplomas framed and mounted on the wall behind her desk. She held both bachelor's and master's degrees in education from The University of Texas in Austin, a highly regarded program for young teachers.

Miss Allen handed Jay's most recent report card to his mother and gave her a minute to review it.

"I will go straight to the point if I may. As you can see, Jay's performance has been, well, shall we say, 'less than stellar?'"

Diane grimaced as she read over the report card. The truth of that statement was quite evident.

"Jay was absent for over a quarter of all the school days. But his citizenship grades give the real clue to his academic performance. He disrupts the class with constant talking, doesn't turn his work in on time, and does not listen attentively. Jay does not make good use of his time."

Diane dropped her head and closed her eyes. "That doesn't surprise me."

"Academically, your son's best subject is arithmetic, in which he earned a B-Plus average. He also performed at the B-level in spelling. His greatest difficulty is reading, where his grades are unsatisfactory."

Diane looked up, expelled her breath, and said, "Yes, I know he doesn't like to read. It's hard for him."

"Well, I'm sure you understand that reading is fundamental to learning. It is the foundation upon which everything else builds."

"I understand. What, uh, what do you think is causing Jay's learning difficulties? And what can be done about it?"

Miss Allen looked off to the left as she clasped her hands together and pressed them to her chin. After pausing for a moment to gather her thoughts, she spoke again. "Well, I am not a doctor or a psychologist, but it seems to me we need to focus on a few specific things first."

"Oh, alright. What would those things be?"

"Okay, well, first, I would say it's essential for Jay to come to school and attend every class daily. He should not miss school unless he is very ill or contagious to other children. He can have a headache or a stomachache here at school just as well as he can at home. But he's got to come to school."

"Yeah, I can see that." Diane said, silently taking the comment as a personal criticism of her parenting skills. "I know I've been pretty lax about letting him stay home from school. I'm sure we can do a better job."

"Good. Second, we need to find some way to keep Jay calm. To slow him down some. Give him a chance to concentrate. Right now, he's like a pinball wildly bouncing off everything and everyone in the room."

Diane hung her head, knowing from experience that this was true. Hearing it from a third person was painful, nevertheless.

"No more sugar, chocolate, or sodas for him."

"But most importantly, you should locate a doctor who may be able to prescribe a medication to help him with this."

Diane raised her head, "A medication? What would that be?"

"Well, as I say, I'm not a doctor, of course, but I have heard some discussion about a condition called 'Hyperkinetic Reaction of Childhood.' Jay's behavior is similar to the symptoms associated with this condition. I presume they have found some helpful medications by now."

"Alright, I guess I can look into that," Diane said, knowing she would not. "Anything else?"

"Yes, third, we need to work on Jay's reading. It would be good if you could read to him daily and have him read to you. The goal is to develop his interest in reading. Read to him things that intrigue him. Help him understand he can experience things vicariously through books that he could never do alone.

"The idea is to try to broaden his mind. Encourage him to think about other possibilities. Find something that's interesting to him, even if it's just *Archie* comic books or *MAD* magazine. The object is for him to discover the value of reading so he will want to do it independently. When he becomes a voracious reader on his own, we will have accomplished our goal, and you will see a radical transformation in his academic performance."

"Oh, that sounds wonderful," Diane said sincerely. "I don't see why we can't do everything you've suggested, and I promise to do my best to help," she said also sincerely, knowing deep down that it wouldn't happen.

"One other thing. It would help if you instilled some discipline in Jay about doing his homework, completing his assignments, and turning them in on time. It's a matter of watching over him and keeping your thumb on him. Keep him focused and disciplined. You need to know what his assignments are so you will know what he has to complete and when."

"I understand. And thank you for your suggestions." *You overly critical bitch. Who are you to talk to me like that?*

"Excellent!" Miss Allen said. "Don't hesitate to contact me if you need any help. Jay is a wonderful boy, and all the other students love him. That's one thing he does well – he makes friends easily."

In time, the 'Hyperkinetic Reaction of Childhood' became known as 'Attention Deficit Disorder (ADD)' and then 'Attention Deficit Hyperactivity Disorder (ADHD).' However, based on what is now understood, Jay's first year of school behaviors were symptomatically consistent with ADHD.

Jay developed this condition beginning in childhood, and it persisted into adulthood, even to this day. Common symptoms of the disorder include being inattentive, impulsive, and hyperactive. In addition, he often experienced absent-mindedness, forgetfulness, difficulty focusing, and problems paying attention. These all could have contributed to his low self-esteem, troubled relationships, and issues at school.

Reading can be difficult and frustrating for those with ADHD because it is hard for them to focus, manage distractions, and process and retain information. As a result, Jay was highly resistant to reading unless the topic was something in which he was truly interested.

CHAPTER SIX

Don't Do the Crime If You Can't Do the Time

"Well, I reckon what this is trying to tell me is,
if you wanna get ahead in life, you gotta break the law."

—— **Jay Emerson**

WHEN I WAS TEN YEARS OLD, it was the era of such crime shows as *77 Sunset Strip, Perry Mason*, and *The Untouchables*. Our family ate Swanson TV dinners on portable TV trays as we watched these programs on a black and white television set with dial knobs and rabbit ears wrapped with aluminum foil. We had our choice of only three network channels in those days – ABC, CBS, and NBC. Color TV was just trying to get a toehold in the industry, but the last show shot in black and white would be only four years later. There was no such thing as Cable TV.

Four Star Productions was the site of the production sets for such shows as *The Rifleman, The Big Valley*, and *Wanted: Dead or Alive*, among many other popular TV programs. The Four Star Studios were practically in my backyard when we lived in Thousand Oaks, and my friends and I often hung out around those sets.

After watching one of these crime-laden shows one night, I stood up and turned to face my mother and father. I said, "Well, I reckon what this is trying to tell me is, if you wanna get ahead in life, you gotta break the law."

I could see the stunned looks come over my parent's faces as they tried to process what I had said. And then, oh, let me tell you, brother, my parents came *unhinged*. I mean, they had a conniption. They began desperately trying to explain all the good and right things about living an honest and lawful life and all the bad and awful things of not.

I thought I had made a rather astute observation. Indeed, it would prove prophetic in my life.

As I got older, I found my father to be more intelligent than I had previously realized. He said one thing that resonated with me, "Son, I don't care what you do, but whatever you choose to do, do it like a man."

Within the context of my apparent criminal aspirations, I took that to mean if you're going to break the law, stand up to it. And, when you are punished, take it like a man. In the colloquial, my father was trying to say, "Don't do the crime if you can't do the time."

"And believe me, son, there will come a day of reckoning."

CHAPTER SEVEN

A Normally Dysfunctional Family

"Whole lotta [swingin'] goin' on."

— Jerry Lee Lewis (Adapted)
Whole Lot of Shakin' Goin' On

I WAS DEVOTED to my mother and trusted her implicitly. She was a dedicated Methodist. Later in life, she saw the beauty and love of Buddhist worship, meditation, and chanting style, so I called her a 'Methodist-Buddhist.'

In 1960, soon after my parents had divorced, my mother took my siblings and me to a Methodist revival meeting in Longview, about eighty miles to the southeast. There was much preaching and praying going on in that circus-sized tent. Other than the spectacle of the thing, these goings-on held no great interest to me. After all, I was only seven years old, so I didn't pay much attention.

However, I do recall hearing one of the pastors talking about 'when the dove sings,' or some shit like that. I wasn't exactly sure what that meant, but anyway, it caught my attention for some reason. The pastor did explain that to Christians, the dove symbolizes the Holy Spirit.

While I could see the image the pastor was trying to create, I didn't quite understand how it applied to me. *When the dove sings? Huh?* I guess it went right over my head because I had no experience with that sort of thing, as far as I knew.

Now that I have gained some education in these matters, I know that the Pastor was referring to a Bible verse, Mark 1:10 (NIV), *'As Jesus was coming up out of the water [after being baptized by John in the river], he saw Heaven being torn open and the Spirit descending on him like a dove.'* In the Bible, a dove symbolizes reconciliation, hope, peace, love, devotion, purity, grace, gentleness, salvation, holiness, and divinity.

But why did I need to hear this? I wondered. *He sure seemed to think it was necessary.*

Now, I don't mean to mislead you. The Emersons may sound like a pretty reasonable family; however, you should know we deliberately kept many things buried under the covers to keep them unknown to the outside community, as did many families in the Fifties, Sixties, Seventies, and even today.

Were we dysfunctional? Only if you consider 'dysfunctional' to include things like unethical business practices, two marriages and two divorces between the same couple, rampant alcoholism, drug addiction, physical and sexual abuse, and felonious criminal activity. But what family wasn't dysfunctional, other than maybe the Cleavers of *Leave It to Beaver* or the Nelsons of *The Adventures of Ozzie & Harriet?* But they had a script to tell them what to do and how to behave.

While my family seemed normal to me, the truth is that we also had a less attractive side.

Putting it simply, I will tell you my older half-brother, Mike, was abusive to me, both physically and sexually. I would have to be wary whenever I walked past his room because he liked to sucker punch me in the stomach every chance he got. I prefer to not discuss the details of the more painful and shameful acts he perpetrated on me.

I will leave that to your imagination. Later in life, Mike would develop some self-destructive behaviors, including an addiction to methamphetamines.

Our family history is replete with drunkards. My maternal grandfather, Richard Cameron, died of alcoholism and complications due to arteriosclerosis. His disease cost him a leg, and he was never the same after that. The loss of one's self, I suppose.

Maybe he drank to either remember the days of his youth or to drown out the voice of his wife, Mildred. Called 'Mimi' by her grandkids, she too was an alcoholic. She had a gene that turned her into *Dr. Jekyll and Mr. Hyde* after only one drink.

I would say we were a somewhat economically affluent family in the Sulfur Springs community. My mother was a member of the Sulphur Springs Country Club, where, in the adapted words of the immortal Jerry Lee Lewis there was a, "whole lotta [swingin'] goin' on."

My mother, Diane Emerson, was what you might call a 'controlled alcoholic.' She self-medicated with Vodka after her cancer diagnosis. She started the days carrying a cup of coffee with a healthy dose of liqueur in it, usually Kahlúa or Bailey's Irish Cream. She drank that all day until happy hour and then switched to cocktails.

It is entirely possible that my observations of my mother's behavior could have contributed to my inappropriate treatment of the women in my life. Who knows? I assume that might have some effect on me, perhaps subconsciously diminishing my respect for women.

My dad, J.M. Emerson, served in the U.S. Navy during World War II, shuttling troops ashore on landing crafts during the D-Day Invasion. After having two boats shot out from under him in combat, he politely declined a third boat. I don't know what the consequences were of him refusing to obey a lawful order. I thought generally the Navy didn't give you that option.

My dad developed what would today be called 'Post Traumatic Stress Disorder,' or 'PTSD'.[2] During the world wars, the condition was known under various terms, including neurasthenia, a condition that is characterized especially by physical and mental exhaustion usually with accompanying symptoms (such as headache and irritability). It is of unknown cause but is often associated with depression or emotional stress and is sometimes considered similar to or identical with 'chronic fatigue syndrome,' 'shell shock,' 'war nerves,' and 'combat neurosis.' The term 'post-traumatic stress disorder' came into use in the Seventies, in large part due to the diagnoses of U.S. military veterans of the Vietnam War.

After the war, J.M. worked as a used car salesman, where he was as dishonest as the day was long. He cheated on his taxes, and the community knew well that he cheated his customers. The local newspaper even published an article about how he was unethical in his dealings. How many used car salesmen would want that kind of publicity following them around?

He played poker and loved to go to Las Vegas. He delighted in enlightening and regaling his friends at the bar and buying everyone a round. He was a 'happy drunk,' you might say. But, of course, the money he spent to buy those drinks could have paid for our family's rent, food, and utilities.

My sister Laury regarded our father as a racist bigot.

It is possible that his PTSD led to his becoming an alcoholic. My father died of alcohol-induced liver cirrhosis with related heart disease. Most assuredly, there was not a whole lot of Jesus in him.

This rampant alcoholism took a terrible toll on multiple generations and branches of my family. Psychologists say being around alcoholics does not provide an affirming environment for children, and that alcoholic parents do not respond to their children appropriately. My siblings and I knew our parents loved us, but they did not relate to us in a way that built us up. Our eventual outcomes evidenced this.

Each of these behaviors tossed stones into the lake of my life and caused many far ranging ripples, the consequences of which could not necessarily be foreseen.

CHAPTER EIGHT

Kidnapped!

"Jay, get up. And get Pete and Laury up, too.
Take them out to that cab outside.
Hurry, quick, quick, quick!"

—— **Diane Cameron Emerson**

DADDY HAD GONE TO TEXAS to find a job and a house. He was preparing for us to meet him when he settled in. Mike had already started college and moved away from home. I was sixteen, Pete was twelve, and Laury was three. The idea was that we would be one big happy family again. That's what we would be, at least in his mind. Honestly, I didn't know what could happen to make that a reality. My mother clearly didn't have that outcome in her plans.

At 4:00 a.m. on the morning we were scheduled to leave California for Texas to meet up with Daddy, my mother entered my room and shook my arm, saying, "Jay, get up. And get Pete and Laury up, too. Take them out to that cab outside. Hurry, quick, quick, quick!"

"What? Why? Where are we going?!"

"Don't worry about it. I'll explain everything on the way. Just hurry."

My mother's strange behavior filled my mind with suspicion and questions because, in the shadows behind her, I saw the figure of a man – the silhouette of Wayne, our mother's latest boyfriend, and an unpopular guy around our house.

Nevertheless, as my mother had instructed, I gathered Pete and Laury. After all, I trusted her. She was my mother. I assumed she knew what she was doing and that she had our best interests in mind, whatever that was.

"Come on. Y'all get in the cab. Hurry up!" I said.

When we got to the taxi, we encountered Wayne loading some apparently hastily packed luggage into the trunk.

"Oh, shit," I groaned. I didn't know Wayne well, but I knew him well enough to know I didn't like him. Also, he was much younger than my mother, who was thirty-seven then. He was in his early twenties.

Nevertheless, the three of us piled into the cab's back seat. My mother climbed into the front seat beside the driver, and Wayne followed her. As the driver drove off, my mother told us she was leaving our dad, and we were going with Wayne to Canada, Prince Edward Island, specifically.

Fuck! With Wayne?

He hadn't specifically done anything to me, but he was only a few years older than me and here he was bonking my mother. That was pretty hard for me to choke down. Besides, he was dumb as a rock. He had no job, no money, no car, and no place of his own.

The driver took us to Los Angeles International Airport. We boarded a nine-hour red-eye flight to Charlottetown Airport in Prince Edward Island with a two-hour layover in Toronto. In those days, an American citizen could pass through Canadian immigration with only a valid U.S. driver's license, or in this case, a mother vouching for her children.

Prince Edward Island was a bleak, gray fishing village. It seemed like a foreign planet to me. So long, sunny Southern California. And so long, Dad.

We stayed on the island off the New Brunswick and Nova Scotia coasts for a few months. Then, we relocated to New York to stay with Wayne's mother in her apartment.

After only a few weeks in New York, I had had enough of constantly being rubbed the wrong way by the mere existence of Wayne in our lives. So, I decided to run away to be with my dad again. I knew I could count on him. He had always been there for me. So, I called him in California.

"Hey, Daddy, listen, I need some help. I wanna come home. Can you help me, please?"

"You want to come home? With me?"

"Yeah. With you. I can't stand it here another minute. Wayne is a raging asshole."

"Well, where are you now?"

"We're living with Wayne's mother in New York. And I don't like her either."

"Does your mother know you want to leave?"

"No, I haven't told her, but I really need to get out of here."

"Okay. I'll see what I can arrange. Call me back in an hour."

"Thanks, Daddy."

"Anything for you, Son. I'm grateful you called on me."

In short order, my dad arranged for a plane ticket for me to fly back to Los Angeles from LaGuardia Airport.

On the day of my flight, I told my mother I was going out to a movie. Instead, I walked to a nearby convenience store and called a taxi to take me to Penn Station. From there I took the E train to the Jackson Heights-Roosevelt Ave station and transferred to a bus that took me directly to LaGuardia Airport. I boarded a nine-hour flight to Los Angeles with a one-hour stopover in Dallas. I left with only the clothes on my back and very little money in my pocket.

My mother got worried when it became late, and I had not returned from the movies. I imagined her mind spinning as she panicked – New York City! Ghettos! Gangs! Crime! I'm sure she imagined me lying unconscious in some alley, mugged, or maybe even dead.

She had no idea where I was or how to contact me.

"Hello, Police?"

"Yes, ma'am. What is your emergency?"

"My teenage son went to the movies this afternoon, and it's almost midnight now, and he is still not home. He should have been here hours ago."

"Yes, ma'am. I understand. What is your name, please?"

"Diane Cameron Emerson," she replied and asked, "Do I have to wait twenty-four hours before I can report him missing?"

"No, ma'am. There is no waiting period for reporting a person missing in New York. In fact, we're doing it right now. I need to collect some information from you about your son. What is his name?"

"Jay Emerson."

My mother provided the answers to all the police operator's questions, and they officially reported me missing.

When I landed in Los Angeles, my father called to tell her I was with him and to assure her I was safe, and everything was alright. I could tell by the expression on my dad's face that she was hopping mad about this.

"So, what did she say?" I asked my dad after he got off the phone.

"Well, putting it politely, as she did not, she is very unhappy about this. She is happy to know that you're okay. But she thinks you betrayed her and that I talked you into doing this."

"But that's not true!"

"I know, Jay, I know. But the good news is that I learned a few new cuss words that I can use in the future."

"HA!" My single syllable belly laugh.

After some time, my mother moved back to Sulphur Springs with Wayne in tow. However, being a New Yorker, Wayne was not well-suited to Texas. Frankly, the local culture didn't take much of a liking to a Yankee gigolo either. So, he took off after only a few months, and, thankfully, that was the end of that unfortunate relationship.

Soon after the kidnapping in the summer of 1969, my parents divorced each other for the second time. The marriage had lasted eight years this time.

While I didn't realize it at the time, my mother's decision to kidnap my siblings and me would be a critical event in my life – perhaps even the jumping-off point for my general downward spiral. My mother had tossed a stone into the water, and the ripple effect from her actions would surely travel far and wide.

CHAPTER NINE

Displaced

"Where am I? And who am I?"

—— **Jay Emerson**

WHILE LIVING IN SOUTHERN CALIFORNIA in the Sixties, I grew up amid the hippie counterculture from Pacific Palisades and Topanga in Los Angeles. The much-maligned long-haired hippies preached free love, promoted flower power, and cautioned against trusting anyone over thirty. They shunned money, materialism, and politics, and repudiated the mainstream values of the times. Hippies experimented with new styles of clothing and music, more relaxed attitudes toward sexual relationships, and recreational use of hallucinogenic drugs, especially LSD and marijuana. They justified the practice as a way of 'expanding their consciousness.' It was the time of sex, drugs, and rock n' roll. And it created a vast new market for the sale of marijuana.

Trying to distance me from these influences, my father sold everything, and moved us to North Dallas. I started my junior year in high school there. This move further turned my world upside down.

I always thought of myself as a friendly, fun kind of guy. I wanted to be popular and have friends. Most teenagers want to attach themselves to a group and assume its self-defined identity. They believe that will bring them approval, acceptance, and a sense of belonging.

In California, I had prided myself in being an athlete, playing high school football and swimming. However, I was not allowed to play football after moving back to Texas because of the mandatory one-year ineligibility for out-of-state transfers. So, I would be a senior before I could play football again. But then, those boys in Texas took that game a little more seriously than did the boys in California. However, I joined the swim team and earned a varsity letter.

So, I was left with trying to figure out who I was, what I was doing, and where I belonged. I had no established self-identity, no role in the community of my peers, no friends, and no girlfriend. In short, I had no 'brand.' I had no reason to believe in, value, or think positively about myself. It all came down to a matter of self-esteem. When you have no self-esteem, you're not concerned about behaviors that are destructive to yourself, others, or your relationships. Destructive behaviors can be a plea for attention.

The move to Texas uprooted me in the middle of my high school years, which can be traumatic for any teenager. I was the new kid in town. My parents had just divorced, my hormones were raging, and I didn't even know what that meant. My father had tossed another stone, and the ripples were spreading.

CHAPTER TEN

The Great White Smuggler

"I'm me, and you should do for me.
Everybody's gonna do for me. I'm gonna get mine.
Y'all may get a little taste, but I will get mine.
Y'all are just gonna get a little taste."

—— **Buck Cameron**

MY COUSIN BUCK CAMERON, the son of Richard Henry and Jimmie Ann Cameron, was a class favorite nominee every year in high school, finally winning the honor as a senior. His girlfriend *du jour* became the homecoming queen that year also.

Buck was selected as All-District in football and named Co-Captain of the Wildcats team. So, it was a big year for him.

My daddy followed Buck's athletic exploits. When we were living in California, he would read news clippings from the local Sulphur Springs newspaper about how well my cousin was doing.

Buck was a sports fanatic and didn't drink or smoke. Yet, while he was a clean-cut athlete, I knew he was also a clean-cut hoodlum. On weekends and evenings, he hung out with his hoodlum friends.

He liked to fight and became accomplished in martial arts during high school. Even though I was still in junior high, that's when I took up martial arts, too. Hell, I idolized my cousin. Everything he did, I wanted to do myself.

Later, as an adult, Buck was by no means monogamous. On the contrary, he believed in having many women in his stable at the same time. However, his first wife, Susan Allen Cameron, didn't tolerate that bullshit. Nevertheless, he was a relentless womanizer, and he would fuck anybody who came within ten feet of him, including all his friends' wives.

Buck's first daughter was Amy Cameron Grant. She was a beautiful young blonde woman. Then, with one of his girlfriends, he had another daughter, Sunny.

Then, Buck had the audacity to bring Sunny to Amy's first wedding and introduce her to everyone. She looked just like Amy, too. It seemed shameful that he would put his illegitimate daughter on display at the wedding of his legitimate daughter and spoil Amy's special day. But that was how Buck rolled.

Amy was the only one who turned out normally after being raised by a family who always hid from the law or served time in prison.

There had been no marijuana at Sulphur Springs High School. So, Buck never smoked a joint and didn't engage in smoking pot until he went to college at North Texas State University.

Then, a pound of grass cost about eighty dollars. Buck envisioned breaking that down, keeping what he wanted, and selling half to three-quarters of it to his friends. As a result, he made more money on selling one pound of pot than he did working all week for Texas Instruments, his regular employer.

Having an entrepreneurial nature, Buck recognized this as a golden business opportunity. Now, he could escalate his smuggling volume almost overnight from pounds to tons.

He was also an ambitious and cunning bastard. He created and became the kingpin of a criminal empire. Cameron drug me and many others into his felonious shenanigans with his persistent and manipulative ways.

Buck's destiny would be to become 'The Great White Smuggler' and a triple-felon sentenced to life without parole.

Larry Daniels

Buck Cameron, Mike and Jay Emerson, and I grew up together, and our parents all ran in the same Sulphur Springs Clique. Buck's family owned the Tanner Furniture and Funeral Home, and mine owned a shoe store and eight leased departments in Northeast Texas, where I worked.

Mike ended up in the Tanner business. That might be because he pursued it, or perhaps because he was the only one left to help keep it going after his grandparents died.

His mother, Diane, also went into the business, not because she wanted to, but because it was the only way to keep the doors open.

We all lived in the same neighborhood. Buck's dad, Richard Henry Cameron, and my daddy were best friends. Richard used to pick up my daddy to go out and carry on their tomfoolery. Our families were close, but in time, my daddy would run off with Richard Henry's wife.

Richard once picked us up in a new Pontiac GTO he had bought for Buck. Richard wanted to show it off, so we got to ride in the car even before Buck did.

Richard was drunk, of course. He was always drunk, a notorious, pitiful alcoholic. Richard didn't imbibe like regular people. When he drank, he would down a whole fifth at a time. That's about twenty-five ounces of liquor or seventeen shots (one and one-half ounces). An average person takes about three to four shots of whiskey to reach the legal blood alcohol concentration (BAC) limit in most states. I've seen him take a fresh bottle of whiskey from the kitchen and walk around half-naked, swigging on it until it was empty. That was the way of his drinking.

The Camerons had a pool table in their house, and we would go there to shoot pool. More times than once, while we were there, Richard would pass out and do a face-plant on the floor in front of us.

Jay's parents and his maternal grandparents were the same way. They were rich and didn't have to answer to anybody because of the Tanner name and the funeral home. So, they got up, drank in the morning, and stayed drunk all day. That's the way it was with that clique of people. Heavy drinking and whoring all the time.

Buck Cameron was a spoiled fuck his whole life. He never had to try hard to get anything he wanted; it always just came to him. If Buck asked for money, he got it. If he asked for a car, he got that.

He was a good student in high school and played football. He was not the school's most popular or best-looking kid, but he expected things to come to him in his privileged state, and they did.

Jay's parents spoiled his half-brother, Mike, the same way but it was not that way for Jay.

Mike's egotistical thinking and belligerent behavior pointed a sharp finger at Jay's nose and showed him how things would be.

Buck ran the show, meaning the marijuana smuggling business, only because he was the one who figured out how to make everything work. He was the only guy who was able to produce the results. Bringing everybody together, they all worked under him, and he was the master. That's the way Buck wanted it.

Imagine Burt Reynold's character, Lewis Medlock, in the 1972 movie *Deliverance*. The clear and undisputed leader of the canoe trip crew – Ed Gentry, Drew Ballinger, and Bobby Trippe – Lewis made all the rules and decisions for the group. Everyone else followed him as if they intuitively recognized him as their natural leader.

Buck Cameron aspired to be the 'Lewis Medlock' in charge of the rest of us.

Buck was Jay's only hero model. And Jay was not alone in that. Buck was the hero for nearly everybody. He was always the influencer, the manipulator, and the ringleader.

Mike, Jay, and the others subordinated themselves to him. Buck was the type of guy people would naturally want to follow. They felt they could trust that he was taking the right path.

We young people make quick decisions, and we don't always analyze things as much as we should because we feel the power. We feel the energy. We think, *This has to be the way to go. Now, I don't have to think for myself anymore.* We follow the leader like minions.

Buck and I got along, but I was not subservient to him. I ran with him for about ten years. Then I pulled away from him while everybody else snuggled up to the 'master.' But he wasn't my master. Cameron was a punk. I would not subordinate myself to a punk.

While Buck was the dominant-aggressive one, Mike and Jay were always lapdogs to him.

Mike was non-aggressive to an extreme degree. He waited for shit to happen because he knew it would. You don't have to do much when you know you'll be fed, have money, drive a new car, and have a beautiful young wife. You play the part, and things will work out. Buck Cameron always played the part. After all, he still had his daddy to fall back on.

However, his daddy died at age forty-five, leaving Buck to fend for himself. There was no longer the option of returning to the well for money. However, he returned to work for Tanner Funeral Home for a while to make some cash between deals.

When Buck went on his criminal way, he got into trouble. Ultimately, now he just scratches along in his old age – broke, empty, and alone.

Buck missed his opportunities in life, and now he's living with the consequences. He had a chance to have it all, but his bad choices cost him everything he already had and everything he might have.

It's unlikely that Jay would have engaged in his future criminal activities without Buck's influence. Jay followed him around like a puppy dog. He used him as a guide, not to emulate him, but because he wanted to go down the same road. Jay said, "I'm gonna follow the money, and this guy's got the money."

Actually, it was all Cameron could do to keep what he had alive. Buck would not obey or follow a leader. He was too arrogant to subordinate himself, and his arrogance got in the way. He never rose to the level of his full potential.

Buck Cameron was a con man in the truest sense of the word. He did what was necessary to have whatever he wanted. He didn't give a fuck if he had to lie, steal, or cheat. Buck was self-absorbed to the *supremus maximus*. He viewed things only through his own eyes.

'Wild Buck' Cameron was born with the proverbial silver spoon in his mouth and still thinks of himself as such to this day. In his mind, he was a much bigger player than he actually was.

Buck's mantra was, "I'm me, and you should do for me. Everybody's gonna do for me. I'm gonna get mine. Y'all may get a little taste, but I will get mine. Y'all are just gonna get a little taste."

CHAPTER ELEVEN

A Life-Long Passion

*"Inhale deeply and hold it
for as long as you can."*

—— **Mike Emerson**

MY COUSIN BUCK and my half-brother Mike were five years older than me. Since Buck attended North Texas State University, he and Mike often hung out there. *Playboy* magazine rated NTSU a top party school back in the Sixties, so the school was the place to go to have a good time.

I idolized my cousin when I was growing up. I thought he was the most awesome guy ever – a 'Big Man.' He was a football hero, martial arts expert, and everything else. There was a lot to admire.

My parents would pawn me off on Mike and Buck. "Take him with you," they would say, "You're going to the school; take him with you. Take him off our hands for a little while."

Buck's dad purchased a brand new 1966 Pontiac GTO muscle car for Buck on his eighteenth birthday. It had a 389-ci V-8 engine with three deuces and a four-speed. The machine was a beast, and I was in lust with it. Having the GTO made Buck seem that much cooler to me.

Though I did not yet have my driver's license when I was fourteen, the GTO was the first car I ever drove. Buck and I were riding around in it one day when he pulled over to the side of the road. He looked at me and said, "You wanna drive, man?"

Without hesitation, I said, "Oh, hell yeah!"

Buck took the passenger seat. I scrambled around the front, trailing my fingertips across the hood, and slid into the driver's seat. The dashboard looked like the cockpit of a fighter jet.

I turned toward Buck and asked, "Are you sure?"

"Yeah, man! Go for it. Just don't kill us in the process."

"I'll do my best, but I can't promise anything."

What could go wrong with an unlicensed fourteen-year-old boy driving a high-powered muscle car?

Depressing the clutch, I turned the ignition key, and the 335-hp engine exploded to life. The dual exhausts rumbled, and the radical cam loped. I gave the accelerator pedal two quick pumps to rev it up, just for fun. The deep, guttural sound the exhausts made was purely sexual.

"AH-HA!" I laughed. A broad grin spread across my face as I caressed the arc of the steering wheel. Gripping the white shift knob with the H-pattern engraved in black, I slipped the transmission into first. Aiming the car down the road, I slammed the gas pedal to the floor, popped the clutch, and that guided missile literally blasted off! The tires threw a spray of gravel, and the rear end fishtailed and then straightened out.

"Hit it, baby!" Buck shouted, grinning at me.

As an unlicensed and untrained driver, I had no idea what I was doing. We were rocketing down the highway when we encountered a curve. A slower vehicle appeared in our lane ahead as we entered the turn. Of course, I didn't have sense enough to brake in that situation.

I looked at the passenger side as we gained on the other vehicle. Buck's face had turned white, and he was jamming his feet hard against the floorboard, leaning back in his seat, trying to stand on an imaginary brake pedal. Buck had such a look of sheer terror on his face; it brought me back to the reality and immediacy of the impending crisis.

At the last second, Buck grabbed the wheel and steered the car into the left lane, and we flew around the slower car at an incredible rate of speed.

"Oh, my God! What a rush!" I screamed.

"Okay. Ride's over, asshole!" Buck shrieked, "Pull over and get the hell out of my fuckin' car!"

After he fumed for a while, he eventually calmed down, presumably after all the adrenaline drained out. "Get back in here, you dumb sonovabitch."

I did, and off we went for the rest of our drive. Needless to say, Buck drove from there on.

On another occasion, Buck, Mike, and I were on one of our trips to NTSU. With Buck driving and Mike in the passenger seat, I was in the GTO's backseat. Mike said, "Jay, we're gonna smoke some weed up there. You gonna tell on us?"

"No, I won't tell on you," I said. "Whatever y'all wanna do."

Just knowing my family would even think about smoking pot blew me away. Buck was an athlete – a football player and martial arts practitioner. I considered doing drugs to be inconsistent with his lifestyle. But I thought, *Well, hell. I know these people. They're my family.*

But smoking weed was not my thing. I was an athlete, too.

Nevertheless, being a curious teenager, I wondered what it would be like. So, I took my first hit of marijuana in the backseat of that GTO in a parking lot at the university.

Mike turned to me and said, "Okay, I got a joint ready, but since you ain't never done this before, I'm gonna give you a 'shotgun.'"

"A 'shotgun?' What's that?"

"Just do as I tell you."

Mike lit the joint and motioned with his hand for me to come closer. He turned the joint around and put the lit end in front of his mouth. Next, Mike pulled me forward until my face was directly in front of his. "Open your mouth."

He blew into the lit end of the joint, directing the smoke out the other end straight into my mouth.

"Inhale deeply," he said. "And hold it for as long as you can."

I found I could take in the smoke without choking or coughing.

But then, after throwing up in the parking lot, I swore, "I ain't never doing this shit again."

Mike had tossed a stone and had no awareness of the future effect of this, which was profound.

That was my first experience smoking grass, and I didn't do it again for a long time. But I admired these guys, and they were still doing it. All my friends from high school were doing it too, so I thought, *Well, what the hell? I'll try it again.*

Later, I started smoking grass regularly while hanging out with friends. I heard Buck was making trips to Mexico, bringing in backpacks filled with fifty pounds of grass. Then, he sold it to his connections at NTSU. Buck had cornered the marijuana market at a university with students from all over the United States and the world.

He also acquired product from another student at NTSU named Rob Warner, from Abilene, Texas. Rob later became a minister of the American Sikh movement where he was called Singh Sahib Singh Khalsa.

I could buy a kilo of marijuana from Buck, light some of it up, take the rest to my school, and sell it. Suddenly, I had money, and everyone wanted to be my friend. Problem solved!

This stone thrown by me would be a critical originating event for all things to come.

Kilo bricks were the size of an actual brick you might build a house with, but the Mexicans pressed it down with Coca-Cola, compressing it.

By the time I was a senior in high school, I would skip class and hitchhike the forty or so miles to North Texas State. I would arrive by lunchtime and buy a brick (about thirty-five ounces) of weed from Buck for eighty dollars, product he got from Rob Warner.

With the weed in a baggy inside a brown paper bag carried under my arm, I would hitchhike back to my school in North Dallas. I would sell the pot for ten dollars a lid (ounce) by 3:30 p.m. I pocketed three hundred fifty dollars and made a profit of two hundred seventy dollars. Over time, I accumulated enough money to purchase a used Volkswagen bus – a 'magic bus,' which made the commute to NTSU easy.

I kept flipping my product and raising my profit to the next level. Of course, the more I bought, the better the price I got, which made my business even more profitable. The problem was that I tended to lose everything about every third or fourth time for one reason or another and then had to start all over. The load might be lost, stolen, or captured, or the buyers might not pay. It was always something.

Buck eventually expanded his operation, so they no longer ran fifty-pound backpacks across the border. Instead, they brought back two to four hundred pounds per trip. They went to Acapulco to fill the trunk of a car, the back of a station wagon, or sometimes a truck with a false bottom under a camper shell. Then, they drove it to the Rio Grande River at night.

And that's how it all began for me. At the time, I did not realize marijuana would become my career's focus, my life-long passion, and the path to my life's destruction.

CHAPTER TWELVE

Partners in Crime

"My captors dug a hole that was more like
a vertical cylinder than a grave.
Then they slid my body down into it,
standing me up with my head at ground level.
Were they to decide to shoot me, I would just slump over,
and they would throw dirt on me."

—— **Tim Gallagher**

I HAD SOME GOOD FRIENDS in Coach Austin's Lake Highlands High School (LHHS) physical education class. After graduating, the five of us – Alex Flanders, William Winchester, Shamus Fitzpatrick, Tim Gallagher, and I – became what I loosely called the 'Partners in Crime.' Not that we were all criminals... yet. I just liked the name, and the meaning of the name would evolve. Our group hung out, partied, went to concerts, and did drugs together. Soon, others came into the inner circle to contribute their skills and talents.

One day, I led three friends out of English class. We each had dropped a tab of LSD, then got up and walked right out of the room. The teacher looked at us and said, "Where do y'all think you're going?"

"Well, we're going outside," I said, "It's a lovely spring day, and we're gonna go enjoy it."

So, with all this skipping of classes, you might wonder, "How did I ever graduate from high school?" The fact was that I had missed too many days to graduate from LHHS.

Fortunately, my mother knew the Principal of Sulphur Springs High School. So, she made an agreement with the Dallas Independent School District that if I could finish my senior year in Sulphur Springs without missing any days, I could get an LHHS diploma.

So, I moved back home while I finished high school as a Sulphur Springs Wildcat.

After graduation, my friends and I lived in various apartments around Dallas and worked at menial jobs. We aspiring young men debated what to do with our lives when we grew up. After deep marijuana-induced consideration by all of us, I came up with what I considered to be a downright brilliant idea.

"Hey, y'all, how about this?"

One of my friends wanted to be a musician and practice his art, but he needed a job. So, I said, "Look, man, if I provided you with a pound of grass, you could sell it to your friends and make a profit. Then you could stay home and write all the music you wanted."

Another friend worked for his daddy, which he didn't want to do. So, I convinced him to sell weed to his friends, too.

Eventually, I got everyone working with me in supplying and developing distribution channels for marijuana.

Can you foresee the potential self-inflicted ripples from this stone?

Of course, since we were teenagers, our brains hadn't fully developed yet. As might be expected, there was no consideration that this was an illegal activity, and we would be committing felonies. Were the authorities to catch us, the penalties could be quite severe. We could go to prison. For a long time.

As teenagers, we naturally believed we were invincible and immortal and nothing bad would ever happen to us. Right? Of course! Everybody knows that.

Showing my friends the arithmetic about how much money they could make, it was not hard to convince them that they should use their apartments as stash houses. At these stash houses, we unloaded, weighed, examined, graded, qualified, and then dispersed the product to our buyers in the specific quantities designated.

My friends would get the drippings from the 'master's table,' usually whatever they swept off the floor. That typically gave them a bonus of a couple of pounds they could sell by the lid to make money.

I began developing connections at NTSU through Buck with Little Artie Hammond and Guillermo Desoto, members of the so-called 'Marlin Mafia,' of which Fred Marco was also a member.

Sometime later in East Texas, Little Artie Hammond would take a bullet to the head.

One night, I came home with an eight-hundred-pound load of grass in a pickup with a camper shell. I stopped off at Mama's to get some sleep. I arrived about three o'clock in the morning and went into the house, keeping the marijuana under the camper shell of my truck.

Mama heard me come in, so she got out of bed and decided to make me some breakfast, but she didn't have all the fixings she needed, so she had to take a trip to the grocery store.

She grabbed my keys and took my truck to the store, where she purchased the things she needed.

With the box boy following close behind her, carrying her groceries out to the pickup, she spied the pot in the truck's bed for the first time. Thankfully, she had the presence of mind to have him put all the groceries into the back seat.

Quick thinking, Mama!

After preparing the food, she called me to the kitchen table. Serving my bacon and eggs, my mother said, "You'll never believe what I found while at the grocery store this morning."

My face turned three shades of red. It's funny how mothers know everything. At least now, it was all out in the open, and my mother and I could be honest with each other about my chosen career path.

Tim Gallagher

I was an original member of the Partners in Crime with Jay since high school. In Mexico, once, I went out without a bodyguard and got abducted. I just wanted to go up the mountain to make a goodwill visit to the people who grew our weed. I considered myself to be an outgoing guy who just wanted to meet those people.

Unfortunately, when I was leaving there, they abducted me. Since I was paying off the Mexican Army to help the group when we landed airplanes down there, my abductors were also interested in keeping me alive.

First, though, they beat the shit out of my driver. Afterward, they sent him back with their demand for my return – ten thousand dollars!

My captors dug a hole that was more like a vertical cylinder than a grave. Then they slid my body down into it, standing me up with my head at ground level. Were they to decide to shoot me, I would just slump over, and they would throw dirt on me.

After allowing me some time to stew in my own juices, so to speak, my captors eventually offered me a hand to pull myself out of the hole. I couldn't believe it. All that time I had been in another realm mentally, reflecting on my life.

My driver told my Mexican Army friend, Capitán Rio, about my capture and he sent a military contingent to rescue me. During the operation, my precarious position caught me in a gunfight between my captors and the soldiers. Of course, I was the only one without a gun.

After my rescue, upon returning to the camp, having been held captive for three days, I told Jay my story in great detail. I had been absolutely terrified – the claustrophobia, the threat of being shot, the threat of being buried alive. It really was too much to endure and still retain my sanity. Jay and I cried and hugged and then went on to the next load – another memorable day, nothing more.

On another occasion, I almost dropped an airplane while flying co-pilot on a Beechcraft Queen Air at about fourteen thousand feet. The aircraft utilized an internal ferry bladder – a giant balloon carrying about two hundred gallons of fuel.

The captain was not monitoring the flow from the ferry bladder into the tanks, so they ran dry. As the fuel pressure gauges bobbed up and down, I knew they were losing pressure, and then the port engine cut out. Soon after that, the starboard engine followed suit, leaving us powerless. There was only silence in the cockpit, and we could not start the engines again.

The pilot struggled feverishly to restart while I tried to maintain as much altitude as possible so we would have a longer glide path. Were we to impact, all that one hundred twenty Octane fuel from the bladder would be right there in the cockpit with us.

Finally, I turned on the boost pumps without telling the captain. That blew fuel into the tanks down at the engines, and the port engine caught. The plane almost rotated over because the pilot wasn't expecting that, but we finally recovered at about two thousand feet. Thank God for that!

My father had envisioned me joining his company and becoming well-known to his connections within the logistics business. He expected me to become the 'go-to' guy and the much-needed savior of the company.

But I suffered from significant issues in high school, as we all did. Unfortunately, I became a raging alcoholic while Jay was away in prison.

Chapter Thirteen

Spirit-Filled Hippies

"You know what?
Why don't you phone me from out of state?"

—— **Attorney Hal Jackson**

I AM SINGH SAHIB SINGH KHALSA, or as I am otherwise known, Rob Warner, Doctor of Oriental Medicine. Being a minister of the American Sikh movement, I attempted to bring spiritual consciousness, awareness, and awakening to those I served.

I was a proponent of hallucinogenic drugs, including LSD, peyote, psilocybin (magic mushrooms), and marijuana.

In the Seventies, I was one of the earliest 'Partners in Crime' with Jay Emerson and Buck Cameron on many of their pot smuggling escapades. I did much to participate with and lead these 'Spirit-Filled Hippies,' as we thought of ourselves, on our spiritual journeys.

When I graduated from Cooper High School in Abilene, Texas, in 1968, I read a piece in *Life* magazine about lysergic acid diethylamide, a potent psychedelic called 'LSD' or 'acid.' The effects included intensified thoughts, emotions, and sensory perception. It manifested mental, visual, and auditory hallucinations at high dosages. The article's main objective was to tell a critical story of how crazy, awful, and dangerous this substance was.

My response was, *That's what I want. I want some of that.*

It was difficult to find marijuana in our town in my school days; however, my friends and I occasionally found some, got high, and had tons of fun.

I met someone who had some acid, and I bought a tab from him. On my way home, I came down with cold sweats and verged on having an anxiety attack. I realized I would not have any more acid after I took that one tab. So, I went back and got another one.

At that point, I felt sure this was something I wanted to do, was going to do, and would do again and again. I began taking LSD as often as possible. I dropped acid at least five hundred times over two to three years. I came to believe LSD, or any of the psychedelics, would expand my mind. That would give me a glimpse of things outside my ordinary consciousness.

After graduating high school, I chose North Texas State University for college because I knew more drug connections at NTSU than anywhere else. In college, I got involved with a group of long hairs. Our purpose for taking drugs was to have a spiritual experience.

I believed LSD assisted me in getting rid of some of the curtains or blockages in my mind and ego. This would lead to a deeper reality hidden behind the mind, a place of spiritual awareness.

In 1968, I got arrested for my drug activities, and so NTSU decided they didn't want 'my kind' attending classes at their university, so they kicked me out of school. So much for my academic career.

I thought, *This is the life I like. So, what am I going to do?*

I started buying pot, LSD, and other hallucinogens wherever possible and selling them. I began expanding my network of people with whom I could buy and sell. Over time, I developed my business to the point where I dealt in much larger quantities.

I ran into some old friends and made some new ones smuggling marijuana out of Mexico who would deliver it to me. I was not involved with cross-border business then because I didn't need to be.

Buck Cameron was one of my new friends, and he and I started an enterprise together. Using my connections, we would go to the Mexican border to pick up the drugs on the U.S. side.

An older guy we called 'Uncle Jake' came into our circle. He was older in the sense he was about twenty-nine when I was only nineteen.

He was a drug smuggler, and his father was one too. So, he had a great deal of experience in smuggling marijuana. Uncle Jake's father taught him the trade using 'drug runner' boats, or 'go fast' boats, in the Gulf of Mexico.

It was eye-opening for me to learn the trade from them.

It wasn't long before we started going into Mexico, getting the drugs, and wading across the Rio Grande River. We carried duffle bags full of marijuana on our backs, bringing it into the United States. Once the pot was on the U.S. side of the border, we would load it into secret compartments in campers or trucks or extra gas tanks under the vehicles. Then, we would load it into a car or truck and drive it to the Dallas-Fort Worth area to sell.

Later, we graduated to more sophisticated techniques and larger quantities.

At this point, Jay Emerson and others bought most of the pot we smuggled. They picked it up at NTSU in Denton and sold it wherever. I was not informed about where it went, nor did it matter to me.

On one of our smuggling trips to the border, Uncle Jake, Buck, and I were wading across the river with a load of marijuana when the authorities detected us. The whole operation came apart. They captured some of the product, but we got a good bit of it across and escaped. We managed to transport some truckloads of marijuana back to Denton.

I knew it was crazy to persist with these activities in the face of everything happening.

I called my friend before I got back into town to let him know I was coming. "Man, it's hot as shit here," he said, "We had a big ass bust last night. About fifty dudes got arrested."

So, I called my lawyer, Hal Jackson. "Hal, I understand y'all had a lot of activity last night."

"Yeah, that's right."

"Am I on the list?"

Hal paused momentarily and said, "You know what? Why don't you phone me from out of state?"

Hal Jackson held three bail bonds on me worth more than a hundred thousand dollars, and he just told me to get my ass out of state. *Okay, they're onto me.*

I had been arrested three times for drug offenses, so I was already pretty hot. I was not what you would call a 'model citizen,' and now the police had me on their radar.

The court had voided my first arrest because the cops kicked in the door without a warrant.

On the second arrest, I walked in as the bust was unfolding, and the court dismissed the charges because I was not in possession when arrested.

The officers did find a gram of hashish on me; however, I snatched it out of the officer's hand and shoved it into my mouth.

The cops beat the hell out of me, trying to extract it, but they could not make me open my mouth before I swallowed the hashish.

They charged me anyway, but Hal Jackson got my charges dropped because I had not been present during the arrest. Neither did they want to admit I had grabbed the hashish out of the cop's hand, so I walked.

The third bust happened right before I went on the lam. The statute of limitations ran out on that one, and nothing ever came of it. Similar circumstances always kept me out of prison.

I still did a lot of acid, smoked marijuana, and smuggled. At the same time, I also learned more about meditation, practiced yoga, and pursued a spiritual life.

Our original purpose with this marijuana business was to get high just for fun. Along the way, we came to believe drugs might liberate the minds of the masses and help bring about a much better consciousness among the general populace.

We felt the world was headed for certain destruction. First, because 'The Man' was running everything. There was the military-industrial complex, Richard Nixon, the Vietnam War, and so on. We couldn't stand it. We needed to do something and considered smoking pot as one way to make that happen.

I'm not sure we ever actually affected any of those matters.

The police pressure on me began to get hotter and hotter, and I realized I had to stop.

"Hey, y'all, I need to bail because they're gonna put me in prison if I don't get the hell out of here," I said to Buck and Jay.

So, I turned my connections over to Buck. He developed those and some more of his own, and I left the scene.

A lot happened in those first three years since high school. In 1971, some of my buddies and I went down to Mexico to set up smuggling operations and new routes. We rented a house in Acapulco and waited for others to join us.

After taking some acid one night, I had a vision that I would be arrested. Sure enough, it came to pass. During that trip, the vision told me my life would become very bad if I did not stop taking, selling, and smuggling drugs. Instead, I needed to dedicate my life to spiritual growth.

However, I did not heed this inner voice. Three days later, some men kicked in the door to our house. They kidnapped all of us and held us at gunpoint for seven days until we arranged to pull together the ransom money. My vision while on the acid trip had played out just as I had seen it.

The men who abducted us claimed to be Mexican police, but we were never sure if that was true. We still sported long hair, and we assumed they had observed us around town, picked up on our intentions, and figured they could make some easy cash. Besides, we were not the most discreet-looking people hanging out in Acapulco. Thankfully, some of our friends in Texas pitched in and wired the funds our kidnappers demanded, so they finally let us go.

After being freed, I flew to a little place called Idyllwild in the San Jacinto mountains of Southern California near Riverside. Some of my friends in that part of the country said I could lay low with them until I sorted out my situation.

So, I was hiding out and didn't have a nickel to my name, but I was so deep into the lifestyle I didn't even want a job. So, I spent most of my time reading books on Eastern spirituality, practicing yoga, meditating, and hiking in the mountains.

In 1980, I returned to Texas, still searching for answers to life's big questions. I reunited with Buck Cameron and Jay Emerson and met Denny McCarthy. Old habits are hard to break, so I started doing a little dealing here and there. Those guys had a much larger operation than anything I had ever seen with regard to the volume and frequency of the smuggling operations.

I became a guy who would come up with a few pounds of marijuana and maybe run out to help unload an airplane somewhere in West Texas. I might drive a load back to Dallas or store product in my stash house. I would bring loads home, and we would sort them out and ship them off to wherever.

I was not actively taking part in the smuggling business. I stayed on this side of the border. Buck, Jay, and some others were much more involved in the planning and operations.

I was still pursuing my yoga practices and had quit dropping acid for several years. While psychedelics would show me places inside, I knew I couldn't stay there because when the drug wore off, so did the experience.

Surely, there must be a better way of capturing the spiritual essence of life and living it more fully.

We all thought of ourselves as spirit-filled hippies. Buck Cameron became a follower of 'I Ching,' [3] an ancient traditional Chinese form of cleromancy, or divination by casting lots. The practice seeks knowledge of the future or the unknown through supernatural means, an occultic, standardized process, or ritual. It provides a philosophical taxonomy of the universe, a guide to an ethical life, a manual for rulers, and an oracle of one's personal future.

Buck studied and used *I Ching* to predict what would happen in his smuggling operations. He consulted it to find out if he would win the appeal of one of his convictions. He referred to it again to determine if he would ever be free from prison. In each case, *I Ching* said, "Yes, you will," correctly predicting both outcomes.

Christianity's view of divination is addressed in Deuteronomy 18:10-11 (NIV), "Let no one be found among you who sacrifices his son or daughter in the fire, who practices divination or sorcery, interprets omens, engages in witchcraft, or casts spells, or who is a medium or spiritist, or who consults the dead."

So, from that perspective, divination is false, deceitful, and worthless and is a sin in any form compared to God's truth. It is not harmless entertainment or an alternate source of wisdom.

Yet Buck Cameron followed *I Ching* 'religiously.'

CHAPTER FOURTEEN

Growing Like a Weed

"We fancied ourselves as anarchists subverting
the laws of the United States of America
for the revolutionary ideal of
getting everybody stoned on pot."

—— **Jay Emerson**

AFTER BEING IN THE BUSINESS of smuggling marijuana for several years in the early Seventies, I had accumulated some money and was living high and wide without a care.

My partners and I often observed other people in our line of business exhibiting what might politely be called 'conspicuous consumption.' They bought Rolexes, drove Porsches, wore expensive clothes and 'bling,' had 'trophy women' hanging off their arms, and flashed fat wads of cash.

They wanted everyone to know they were making big money and were not ashamed for people to know the source of that money. Apparently, the attention this brought made them feel special and consequential, likely assuaging their lack of self-esteem.

However, my partners and I played it differently. We never advertised who we were or what we were doing. We weren't into that flash and cash trip because we knew it always drew heat. We never socialized with general society to avoid scrutiny because we wanted to keep everything private and secret – on the 'down low,' so to speak.

So, we led secluded lives as just a bunch of 'spirit-filled hippies.' I took on the image of a cowboy, wearing Wranglers, a western shirt, short hair, the straightest Fifties-era glasses I could find, and drove an El Camino.

We were careful with whom we chose to do business. Unfortunately, we didn't have the advantage of contractual agreements, litigation, or even a Better Business Bureau report to protect us. So, we did not choose our business partners based on their business acumen. Instead, we chose them because they were our friends. After all, we thought we could trust our friends. And we knew that our friends would have our backs no matter what happened, through thick and thin.

Some people can separate their business from friendships, but we did not do that. We would not work with anyone who was not a friend. We had to have that friendship to trust that they would do what they were supposed to do. After all, our health and welfare depended on it, not to mention our lives and our freedom.

In the late Sixties and early Seventies, there were three prominent drug families in the Dallas-Fort Worth area, and Buck Cameron and I, along with our 'Partners in Crime,' were one of them.

Our group was informally but definitively led by Buck Cameron, and the number of participants in our activities alternately grew and shrank. We also partnered with other smugglers as needed.

The Drug Enforcement Agency (DEA) knew Mexican drugs were being transported up Interstate 35 from San Antonio through Austin to the Dallas-Fort Worth Metroplex. Once the drugs reached Dallas-Fort Worth, we distributed them to our dealers, who were always out of state in places like Kansas City, Chicago, Virginia Beach, or New York. We never dealt in our own backyard. The local authorities quietly cut us a little slack because of this. They knew what we were doing, but they silently agreed that as long as we weren't selling in their backyard, it was okay, meaning there was no problem as long as we didn't put their kids at risk.

In the early-Seventies, Guillermo Desoto and his Marlin Mafia connected with the Osmont family in Laguna Beach, California. They scored some pure LSD and brought it back to Texas. We dealt a lot of LSD in those days, along with marijuana. So, everyone was one big happy family.

And then, with the heat bearing down on us, the entire group went on the lam. My girlfriend, Kim, and I joined Guillermo, Buck, and their families. We all went to Guerneville, California, seventy-five miles north of San Francisco, in Sonoma County, where we stayed with some people who owned a motel on the Russian River.

It was a unique opportunity and a glorious time for me. We were all young. That was about the time of Woodstock, and we were all loving and living, happy, and smoking pot. But I know that while I floated along, Buck and Susan, Guillermo and Maria, and all the others there were trying to figure out what the hell we were going to do to get some money and keep on going.

I had no legal reason for running but went along for the adventure. I had no idea what was going on. I was just a teenager, enamored with the lifestyle of 'free, free, free.' We were doing what we wanted, how we wanted, and as we wanted. We fancied ourselves as anarchists subverting the laws of the United States of America for the revolutionary ideal of getting everybody stoned on pot.

We held those early ideals of wanting to improve society until money got involved, and then it all went to hell. We were all good buddies when we were doing fifty-pound loads, but the money made a difference when we started dealing in thousands of pounds. Then, the real agendas began to appear.

In the summer of 1976, Kim got pregnant. Since she was pro-life, she was intent on keeping the baby. And I didn't want to lose her, so I said, "Well, hell, I'll give it a shot." So, she had my son Jeremy Emerson the following year. Do you see that stone skipping across the water? It's light and smooth, so it flies quickly and skips easily, on and on and on.

One of Buck Cameron's brothers-in-law was involved with a group of Mexican pot dealers out of the Rio Grande Valley. Buck introduced Denny McCarthy, also one of Buck's brothers-in-law, to Oscar Morlett of the Morlett Brothers, who drove tractor-trailers to Dallas carrying four to ten thousand pounds of marijuana hidden beneath layers of produce.

Consequently, we developed a monstrous market at that time.

We were making so much money, and there was so much more to be made that eventually, we graduated to flying our product from Mexico into Texas, which allowed us to bring in seven hundred fifty to a thousand pounds per trip.

With this approach, we didn't have to deal with the Highway Patrol or checkpoints. We just flew over the border. We thought airplanes seemed like a good idea, so we started acquiring Piper Cherokee Sixes, Douglas DC-3s, and De Havilland Doves. A Piper Navajo Chieftain was the first plane we bought. It was a two hundred twenty-thousand-dollar plane we could get with a minimal down payment because the person who had it held it under a lease.

There were several options available to us for acquiring airplanes.

We could buy them for cash without anyone being persnickety about us registering the transfer.

We could steal them. The planes did not need a key; they would start if we could just get inside.

Some people who owned planes faced financial issues and risked losing their airplanes through repossession. We could pay these owners to use their aircraft, thus allowing them an opportunity to avoid repossession. The owners usually enjoyed making this arrangement again and again.

We also knew people with planes that would just let us use them. If we crashed or had to destroy the aircraft, the owner would file an insurance claim for a stolen airplane and collect the insurance proceeds.

Buck had accumulated a small fleet of airplanes to fly marijuana over the border, and I wanted to be in the middle of that, if not on top of it.

Buck and Aaron Stanton had relocated to Cuernavaca in the State of Morelos in Mexico, sixty-five miles south of Mexico City. They stayed there, living in the mountains, making connections, and acquiring whatever product they wanted.

In the meantime, I learned the locations of all the airstrips in the area, so I became the liaison. When we went on a cross-border smuggling trip, we typically never told the pilots where we were going. We thought it better that way because the less the pilots knew, the less afraid they were inclined to be.

When we reached the location, I would guide the pilots down to where Buck waited on the airstrip with the merchandise. Usually, we were able to hire Mexican locals to load the plane. The pilot flew the load home to Texas, where our partners served as the landing crews and unloaded everything from the airplane. Then, we delivered the shares to our connections at NTSU. In turn, those connections transported the product to the Northeast, where they sold it. They returned in a week or two, and the process repeated.

In a complex undertaking such as this, the nature of the enterprise dictated separate functions. A conspiracy of such magnitude required financiers, pilots, flight crews, ground crews, loaders and unloaders, mechanics, drivers, message carriers, meeting place providers, and many others.

We all played different roles. I was the logistics guy. I ensured the pot arrived and got stored, weighed, categorized, and dispersed among Buck Cameron's designated customers.

That's how it all started, and everything went reasonably well until the late Seventies.

Rob Warner from Denton introduced me to Denny McCarthy. Denny had been smuggling marijuana on the ground with many other people, but, at the time, Buck Cameron and I were the only ones flying it across the border. Having something of a background in flying, although indirectly, Denny wanted to become involved with us.

So, we took Denny on, and he and I began filling in gaps in the organization. We did support work and ran a warehouse operation where we graded, weighed, and numbered the merchandise. We had one colossal stash house, filling every bedroom floor-to-ceiling with product. We had several other similar stash houses, and later, we went to commercial warehouses when the volumes picked up.

When Denny first became involved with the group, he and I served as 'unloaders,' which meant we helped unload the product from the airplanes into trucks or vans. One of Rob Warner's jobs was to position Airstream travel trailers throughout the United States. We were doing business on both the East and West coasts. These trailers would give us secure places to store products, sleep, and work.

In 1973, Saudi Arabia and other OPEC nations imposed an oil embargo on the United States and other countries to punish us for supporting Israel during the Yom Kippur War. Consequently, historic gas shortages became a reality for all Americans and citizens of other nations.

As a result, President Richard Nixon imposed gas rationing, which allowed motorists to fill their gas tanks on only certain days of the week, depending on whether the last digit of their license plate was an even or an odd number. Even-numbered license plates could buy gas on even-numbered days, and so forth with odd-numbered plates.

Consequently, panic and chaos ensued. Gas stations ran out of gas, lines of cars whose owners waited to buy gas extended for blocks from every service station, cars frequently ran out of gas while waiting in line, tempers flared, and fights and shootings occurred among the drivers.

Despite that, Denny and I were responsible for fueling and maintaining a fleet of cars running from Dallas to New York. These were big Ford LTDs, Chevrolet Caprices, and Chrysler New Yorkers – anything with massive trunk space that could accommodate a large load of marijuana. These vehicles had trunk space averaging twenty cubic feet – as big as a refrigerator! We had a whole collection of these gas guzzlers scattered all over Dallas.

So, Denny and I kept the cars' tanks full of gas and their trunks full of merchandise while we waited for the drivers from up north to pick them up. Denny and I would move them from one apartment complex to the next, keeping them full of gas and swapping out their license plates depending on the day of the week.

The business was literally growing like a weed. No pun intended. Well, maybe just a little one.

Act Two

DOING THE CRIME

CHAPTER FIFTEEN

The War on Drugs

"Casual drug users should be taken out and shot."

—— Los Angeles Police Chief Daryl Gates

The War on Drugs [4] was a phrase used to refer to a government-led initiative that aimed to stop illegal drug use, distribution, and trade by dramatically increasing prison sentences for both drug dealers and users. The movement started in the Seventies and is still evolving today. Over the years, people have had mixed reactions to the campaign, ranging from full-on support to claims that it has racist and political objectives.

The War on Drugs Began

Drug use for medicinal and recreational purposes has been happening in the United States since the country's inception. In the 1890s, the famous *Sears and Roebuck Catalogue* included an offer for a syringe and a small amount of cocaine for a dollar-fifty. At that time, cocaine use was legal.

Some states passed laws to ban or regulate drugs in the 1800s, and the first congressional act to levy taxes on morphine and opium took place in 1890.

The Smoking Opium Exclusion Act in 1909 banned possession, importation, and use of opium for smoking. However, opium smokers could still use it as a medication. This act was the first federal law to ban the non-medical use of a substance, although many states and counties had banned alcohol sales previously.

In 1914, Congress passed the Harrison Act, which regulated and taxed the production, importation, and distribution of opiates and cocaine.

Alcohol prohibition laws quickly followed. In 1919, the country ratified the Eighteenth Amendment, banning the manufacture, transportation, or sale of intoxicating liquors, ushering in the 'Prohibition Era.' The same year, Congress passed the National Prohibition Act (aka, the Volstead Act), which provided guidelines on federally enforcing Prohibition.

Prohibition lasted until December 1933, when the country ratified the Twenty-First Amendment, overturning the Eighteenth.

Marijuana Tax Act of 1937

In 1937, Congress passed the 'Marihuana [sp] Tax Act.' This federal law placed a tax on the sale of cannabis, hemp, or marijuana.

While the law didn't criminalize the possession or use of marijuana, it included hefty penalties if users didn't pay the taxes, including a fine of up to two thousand dollars and five years in prison.

Controlled Substances Act

President Richard M. Nixon signed the Controlled Substances Act (CSA) into law in 1970. This statute called for the regulation of certain drugs and substances.

The CSA outlined five 'schedules' used to classify drugs based on their medical application and potential for abuse.

Schedule One drugs were considered the most dangerous, as they posed a very high risk for addiction with little evidence of medical benefits. The list of Schedule One drugs included Marijuana, LSD, heroin, MDMA (ecstasy), and other drugs.

The substances considered least likely to be addictive, such as cough medications with small amounts of codeine, fell into the Schedule Five category.

Nixon and the War on Drugs

In June 1971, Nixon officially declared a 'War on Drugs,' stating that drug abuse was 'Public Enemy Number One.'

A rise in recreational drug use in the Sixties likely led to President Nixon's focus on targeting some types of substance abuse. As part of the War on Drugs initiative, Nixon increased federal funding for drug-control agencies and proposed strict measures, such as mandatory prison sentencing, for drug crimes. He also announced the creation of the Special Action Office for Drug Abuse Prevention (SAODAP).

Nixon created the Drug Enforcement Administration (DEA) in 1973. This agency was a special police force committed to targeting illegal drug use and smuggling in the United States.

At the start, Congress gave the DEA one thousand four hundred seventy special agents and a budget of less than seventy-five million dollars. Today, the agency has nearly five thousand agents and a budget of over two billion dollars.

Ulterior Motives Behind War on Drugs?

During a 1994 interview, President Nixon's domestic policy chief, John Ehrlichman, provided inside information suggesting that the War on Drugs campaign had ulterior motives, which mainly involved helping Nixon keep his job.

In the interview, Ehrlichman explained that the Nixon campaign had two enemies: 'the antiwar left and black people.' His comments led many to question Nixon's intentions in advocating for drug reform and whether racism played a role.

Ehrlichman said, "We knew we couldn't make it illegal to be either against the war or blacks, but by getting the public to associate the hippies with marijuana and blacks with heroin, and then criminalizing both heavily, we could disrupt those communities. We could arrest their leaders, raid their homes, break up their meetings, and vilify them night after night on the evening news. Did we know we were lying about the drugs? Of course, we did."

The Seventies and The War on Drugs

In the mid-Seventies, the War on Drugs took a slight hiatus. Between 1973 and 1977, eleven states decriminalized marijuana possession.

Jimmy Carter became president in 1977 after running on a political campaign to decriminalize marijuana. During his first year in office, the Senate Judiciary Committee voted to decriminalize up to one ounce of marijuana.

Say No to Drugs

In the Eighties, President Ronald Reagan reinforced and expanded many of Nixon's War on Drugs policies. In 1984, his wife, Nancy Reagan, launched the 'Just Say No' campaign, intending to highlight the dangers of drug use, primarily for America's youth.

President Reagan's refocus on drugs and the passing of severe penalties for drug-related crimes in Congress and state legislatures led to a massive increase in incarcerations for nonviolent drug crimes.

In 1986, Congress passed the Anti-Drug Abuse Act, which established mandatory minimum prison sentences for certain drug offenses. This law was later heavily criticized as having racist ramifications because it allocated longer prison sentences for crimes involving the same amount of crack cocaine (used more often by black Americans) as powder cocaine (used more often by white Americans). Five grams of crack triggered an automatic five-year sentence, while it took 500 grams of powder cocaine to merit the same punishment.

Critics also pointed to data showing that law enforcement targeted and arrested on suspicion of drug use people of color at higher rates than whites. Overall, the policies led to a rapid rise in incarcerations for nonviolent drug offenses, from fifty thousand in 1980 to four hundred thousand in 1997. In 2014, nearly half of the one hundred eighty-six thousand people serving time in federal prisons in the United States were there for drug-related charges, according to the Federal Bureau of Prisons.

A Gradual Dialing Back

Public support for the war on drugs waned in later decades. Some Americans and policymakers feel the campaign was ineffective or led to a racial divide. Between 2009 and 2013, some forty states took steps to soften their drug laws, lowering penalties and shortening mandatory minimum sentences.

In 2010, Congress passed the Fair Sentencing Act (FSA), which reduced the discrepancy between crack and powder cocaine offenses from 100:1 to 18:1.

The recent legalization of marijuana in several states and the District of Columbia has also led to a more tolerant political view on recreational drug use.

Technically, the War on Drugs is still active, but with less intensity and publicity than in its early years.

CHAPTER SIXTEEN

The Lamesa Operation

"Sometimes you just gotta take the leap and then build your wings on the way down."

—— **Jay Emerson**

GEORGE JAMESON was a progressive individual, a 'Man's Man.' You might call him a 'smooth operator,' not a hustler, not J. Crew, but a classy, *Playboy* magazine-type guy.

In the Seventies, the Village in Old Town was an apartment complex near the Northwest Highway in Dallas. The apartments were the 'In' place to live and were known as a 'Swinger's Paradise.' This debonair bachelor lived there and operated a car wash nearby at Lovers Lane and Greenville Avenue.

Additionally, he owned a dealership for Bill Bennett's Delta Wing Kites and Gliders. They were among the first manufacturers of light, non-motorized, foot-launched, heavier-than-air aircraft wings in the U.S. The company helped develop the basic design of modern flyers, added features such as emergency chutes and mylar-coated sail cloth, and improved handling and performance.

At that time, I was a spirited young man strongly inclined toward marijuana smoking and smuggling. One Saturday afternoon, I stopped in at George's car wash. On one wall of the waiting room was a poster showing a man using one of these gliders – no shirt, no shoes, and he was literally flying! The words at the bottom said, "Do you want to fly?"

"Well, hell, yeah! I've always wanted to fly," I said out loud. Since I was six, I flew vicariously through my TV with *Adventures of Superman*, *Whirlybirds*, and *Sky King*. I thought, *I can do that*.

By the end of the weekend, I had bought a hang glider. And naturally, George offered lessons, so I took him up on his offer.

He took me to the dam on Lewisville Lake near Denton and pushed me off. I landed, busted my ass, got back up, ran to the top of the hill. "Let's do it again!"

I was not afraid of anything. My life philosophy was, "Sometimes you just gotta take the leap and then build your wings on the way down."

That day, I turned all my friends on to this thrilling and extraordinary sport. In short order, we all bought a hang glider and were soaring like eagles.

After that, I once flew a single-seat Ultralite aircraft powered by a small engine from Sulphur Springs to a friend's house in Weatherford, about one hundred forty miles away. Due to the distance, I had to land on a football field in Mesquite to refuel along the way. I even wore a black scarf around my neck à la Snoopy (except his scarf was red.) It was an incredible experience, and I was an adrenaline junkie.

In addition to being a playboy and owning a car wash and a hang gliding dealership, George Jameson was a good pilot.

Like any other young man in the Seventies, he was a 'credit card millionaire,' leveraged to the hilt, the owner of a beautiful new airplane, and had no idea how he would make the payments.

Seeing possible benefits for both of us and being the silver-tongued devil I was, I approached him with a proposition. "Hey,

George, with your awesome piloting skills, have you ever considered flying marijuana? For fun and profit?"

He never had but was not opposed to the idea. So, I introduced him to it, and he proved to be an outstanding smuggler pilot.

So I went to my cousin, Buck Cameron, the ringleader of our pot smuggling operation, and said, "Hey Buck, I hear you need someone to fly your airplane."

In 1974, when I was twenty-one, Cousin Buck master-minded a plan for George and him to use a twin-engine Piper Navajo Chieftain to carry a fifteen-hundred-pound load of marijuana from Mexico to a remote airstrip in Texas.

The Lamesa Municipal Airport sat about two miles northeast of the city limits of Lamesa, a farming and oil and gas-producing community sixty miles south of Lubbock, Texas, on the Llano Estacado. It was close enough to land on if you still had fuel after crossing the border.

Bert Freeman had been the best friend in high school of Susan Allen Cameron, Buck's first wife. In general, he was nothing more than a teenage hanger-on who just wanted to get stoned. Buck instructed Bert and me to drive a pickup from Dallas to meet George, him, and the plane at the airport in Lamesa. There, we would pick up the product and bring it back to our stash houses.

We became frantic when we arrived in Dallas to switch to the pre-arranged white Chevy dually with a camper shell. Susan was late cleaning and scrubbing the truck of all identity and trash, which she was supposed to have done before we got there. So, Bert and I had to finish the job for her.

The trip to the rendezvous point was about three hundred twenty miles, more than a five-hour drive. Bert and I would drive to Lamesa through Dallas and Fort Worth rush hour traffic, compounding our frustrations.

Dammit! We're gonna be late!

We expected Buck and George to land about ten o'clock, but Bert and I were nowhere around at that time and were still hours away. They couldn't have known what was happening, where we were, or when we would be there.

Then, suddenly, the proverbial light bulb glowed above George's head. "Maybe we should try to rent a U-Haul truck. We'll load everything up here and drive it out."

That sounded like an excellent idea to Buck. So, he called a taxi from a pay phone at the airport to pick them up and take them into town.

They rented a van from the only U-Haul dealer they could find that was still open in the wee hours of the morning. Rental Manager Ralph Henry was happy to break up his uneventful evening to serve them.

Lamesa was the county seat of Dawson County with a population of about eleven thousand, two-thirds of which were Hispanic, for the most part, illegal aliens and itinerate farm workers. Besides farming, there was a booming oil business (or 'bidness' as real Texas oilmen would say) in the area. The local petroleum operations, which operated twenty-four-seven, often needed to rent trucks, trailers, or tools at any hour of the day or night. So, it would not be unusual to find a rental place open this late in that environment.

Having completed their transaction, Buck and George prepared to leave the dealership in the rented van. Just then, the manager happened to mention that he, too, was a pilot. He lit a Chesterfield

Kings non-filtered cigarette and said, "It seems kinda strange that y'all would need a truck like this in the middle of the night."

"Really?" Buck said. "Aren't you open now so you can provide U-Hauls like this to people like us in the middle of the night?"

Ralph Henry puffed on his cigarette and said, "Well, I reckon you got me there. But most people who do that are in the oil 'bidness.'"

George said, "So, it's like this, you see. We're an independent freight line flying for Texas Instruments, and we've got some critical parts to deliver to some Aggies." That was their story, anyway. "We have to get these parts there by the deadline, or else we risk defaulting on the contract."

The manager tossed his butt on the ground and snuffed it out with the toe of his boot. Smiling out of one side of his mouth, he said, "Hmm… Good story. But isn't TI in the DFW Metroplex somewhere?"

"Yes, it is. We flew out of Love Field in Dallas."

"Yeah. And isn't Texas A&M in College Station?"

"That's true, too."

"Well, if I remember my geography right," Henry said, "The university is about one hundred eighty miles south of Dallas."

"You're batting a thousand so far."

"I know that Lamesa is about three hundred miles or so west of Dallas.'"

"Still winning."

"Yeah." Ralph, an obvious chain smoker, pulled the soft pack out of his breast pocket and lit another cigarette. He noticed George staring at his actions. So, Ralph held the fresh Chesterfield Kings out toward George and said, "Preferred by professional smokers."

George quickly looked away, and his face flushed with embarrassment at being caught.

"So, what the hell are you doing out here?" Ralph asked. "The way I see it, you're about four hundred miles off course."

"Yep, that sounds about right," George said.

"You should have gone south instead of west."

George nodded his head in agreement. So much for their official story.

"Well, you know, there's been a lot of avionics and navigation stuff stolen from planes at the airport recently." The manager looked up from the ground and said, "So maybe I'll call a fellow I know who kind of watches out for us all and have him run out there and check up on everything."

With that, Buck and George took their van and hightailed it back to the plane.

After Ralph told Dawson County Sheriff Charlie Henry all he knew and what he suspected, Charlie said, "Okay, I'll go see about it, but it'll be a little while. I'm kinda tied up right now."

Twenty minutes later, Sheriff Charlie grabbed his cowboy hat and he and his partner headed for the airport. Having been alerted to the possibility that he might come upon some kind of drug smuggling operation, Charlie ordered two other units to follow as back-ups.

The short drive from the U-Haul place to the airport gave Buck and George an almost thirty-minute head start. When the County Sheriff and the other officers arrived, they had already transferred all the marijuana from the airplane to the rented U-Haul van.

Buck and George were pulling out of the terminal when they passed by Charlie's patrol car just as he drove in. Charlie recognized the van, made a quick U-turn with his cruiser, switched on the light bar, and pulled the boys over. The backup vehicles pulled up and blocked the van's escape path.

After reporting the stop on the radio, the Sheriff approached the rented van. He was a big, heavy, tall man with a bulbous belly, and a leather holster for his .45-caliber service revolver hanging off his belt. He pointed his gun and a flashlight. "DRIVER! PUT YOUR HANDS OUT THE WINDOW WHERE I CAN SEE 'EM."

"We ain't armed!" Buck called out, extending his arms through the window.

"Step out of the vehicle, please. Very slowly."

Buck obeyed, and Henry spun him around, jerked his arms behind his back, and secured him with shiny silver metal handcuffs. "Now, sit down on the ground and cross your legs Indian style."

The Sheriff looked the van's cab and motioned with his hand for George to come out. "Now, you, slide over here and come out the driver's side door."

When he complied, the Sheriff neutralized him in the same fashion.

After searching both men for weapons, he loaded them into his cruiser's backseat. "May I have your permission to search your vehicle?"

"Only if you have a warrant," Buck said.

"I think I can arrange that. In the meantime, y'all make yourselves comfortable."

At the Sheriff's instructions, one of the deputies headed back into town to arrange for a search warrant.

In the meantime, Sheriff Henry walked around the van, and when he reached the back door, he smelled the presence of marijuana. He grinned at his partner and said, "I've heard about these 'late-night tree toppers,' and, by God, I believe we have one of 'em right here in front of us."

In short order, the deputy returned with the search warrant and handed it to the Sheriff.

The Sheriff glanced over the document and then said, "Alright, we got 'em."

Charlie watched his partner cut the lock off the van's rear door with bolt cutters. They discovered the fifteen hundred pounds of weed when they rolled up the door. So, the Sheriff arrested Buck and George and read them their rights.

"Muñoz, Gutiérrez, y'all take these two Yahoos to County, book 'em, and lock 'em up."

Henry walked over to his squad car and spoke through the window, "What kind of aircraft did you gentlemen fly in here?"

"A twin-engine Piper Navajo Chieftain," George said.

"What's the tail number?"

"N4217D."

"Okay, Longoria and Benson, y'all unload this stuff, impound the van, the contraband, and the airplane, which is over at the terminal. Here's the type of plane and the tail number," he said, handing Longoria a note with that information. "When you've done all that, take the marijuana to the station and lock it up in the vault."

"Hey, Sarge," Buck casually asked, "If you don't mind my asking, are you any relation to the Henry over at the U-Haul dealer? I believe his name was Ralph."

"Oh, yeah, Ralph. He's my older brother. Good man, that Ralph."

Bert and I were about two hours behind schedule to reach our destination when we made it through the Metroplex traffic. Arriving in the pitch black dark at about two in the morning, I could see the lights of an aircraft on the end of the runway. It was revving up his engines in preparation for taking off.

Great! They're still here! But what are they doing there?

I drove the truck onto the taxiway, flashing my headlights. I parked just off to the side of the runway, hoping they had seen me. I also clicked the air-to-ground radio to say, "It's me!"

We could hear the engines revving. *They're taking off! Wait! We're here!*

As the plane rolled down the runway, it passed in front of our truck's headlights. *Oh, hell! That's not our plane!* Different pilot, different plane. *Where the hell is our airplane?*

At that moment, the headlights and rooftop emergency lights of the Sheriff's vehicle came on and approached us. We sat still, watching, confused, wondering *what the hell is happening?*

When the Sheriff got within yards of us, the plethora of his lights blinded us.

Well, shit! This can't be good.

When Bert and I had arrived, the police were still on the scene, completing their investigation and paperwork. So, they pulled us over and asked, "What are y'all doing out here?"

Well, hell, I thought, *okay.*

Sheriff Henry threw me up against his squad car. His fat belly weighed heavily on my back as he cuffed me.

He said, "Well, boys, we need to see what you got in your pockets."

I had a beautiful woven Indian pouch containing four joints, which he discovered. He went to the dually truck, which Buck's wife was supposed to have cleaned out. Instead, he found a picture of Buck and his father, Richard Henry Cameron, in a nice eight-by-ten wooden frame under the front seat. I guessed we missed that because we hadn't taken the time to be thorough enough.

"Hey!" The Sheriff exclaimed, "We just busted this guy about two hours ago. And you're saying you don't know these people?"

He motioned to the other officers, "Lock 'em up! Obviously, they're all cohorts."

The court found Buck Cameron and George Jameson guilty of possessing fifteen hundred pounds of marijuana with intent to distribute. It sentenced them each to eighteen months in prison.

Buck went on the lam before he was due to report.

That was my first bust. Sheriff Henry had charged Bert and me with possession of the weed. Bert and I hired Attorney Jack George Milner to represent us.

At trial, Milner asked, "Sheriff Henry, can you tell me the exact moment when my clients possessed this marijuana?" After a short pause and no answer from the Sheriff, he continued, "No? Is that because two hours before my clients even arrived on the scene, you had already locked up the marijuana in your vault at the police station?" He paused to let that sink in. "So how could my clients have had possession?"

The judge threw out the case. The Sheriff had indicted us with the wrong charge, not for conspiracy to distribute but for possession. So, Bert and I both got off scot-free.

That was too easy, I thought.

The judge had set me off in an unfortunate direction. He threw a stone, the ripples of which gave me an unwarranted and dangerous sense of confidence.

On the other hand, we had lost fifteen hundred pounds of weed, which meant we owed some Mexicans. We knew they would ask us to explain what had happened. They understood but still didn't want to take the loss. They knew we were good people, so they fronted us more product to help us build ourselves back up so we could pay them off ¡*ahorita!* meaning 'right now!'

Nevertheless, instead of taking this near conviction as a sign, I did not leave the business as rational people would have done after their first bust. Anyone with half a brain would have said, "Okay. That's it for me. I'm outta here." Instead, I continued on for years to come.

CHAPTER SEVENTEEN

The Colombia Operation

Cocaine

"Cocaine is poison."

—— **Pablo Escobar**
(The King of Cocaine)

IN AN ATTEMPT TO ERADICATE the importation of cannabis into the United States, in 1970, the American government offered helicopters, airplanes, and money to Mexico. In return, the U.S. requested that their southern neighbor use the matériel to spray an herbicide on all marijuana crops across their countryside. This would prove to be a large stone tossed into our lake.

The Americans allowed the Mexican officials their choice of chemicals. The Mexicans chose paraquat, which killed green plant tissue on contact and was tasteless, odorless, and invisible. Of course, anything poisonous enough to kill plants would also be equally toxic to humans. Only a well-trained eye could identify leaves that had been sprayed with paraquat.

Despite knowing that this toxin concentrated in the lungs when ingested and could be fatal in even tiny amounts, the State Department accepted Mexico's poison of choice. The United States delivered the promised helicopters, airplanes, and at least sixteen million dollars in U.S. taxpayer funding.

The stated intent of this program was to destroy the cannabis at its source by spraying the fields. However, it is important to understand that for a grower in impoverished Mexico, not harvesting marijuana could yield an annual income of just two hundred dollars. Whereas, harvesting marijuana could mean earning a yearly income of five thousand dollars! Consequently, many growers harvested the poisoned weed and shipped it north anyway. Ripples from the original large stone.

Three days later, Denny McCarthy was up in the mountains with one of the growers when a couple crop dusters approached. "Hey, man! They're gonna come over here and spray all your crops!"

The grower said, "Nah. They ain't coming over here."

"No? Well, they're heading right this way."

"I'm telling you, man, it ain't gonna happen."

Sure enough, the planes veered off when they reached the grower's valley. Later, on that same trip, McCarthy witnessed the grower making a payoff to the Mexican police.

That's how it's done in Mexico – '*la mordida,*' the bribery.

When the Mexicans started killing the marijuana crops, we had nothing for two seasons in the mid-Seventies. The product we did get had that poison on it. No one wanted to smoke it, and we didn't want to sell it. Since none of us worked a straight job, we had no money coming in, and it soon got to the point where we were all starving.

When we first organized our business years earlier, we agreed to maintain certain standards, including not dealing with people involved with cocaine. Those people were all about guns. We never carried weapons and didn't work with people who did. Even Pablo Escobar, the founder and sole leader of the Medellín Colombia Drug

Cartel, also known as 'The King of Cocaine,' said, "Cocaine is poison."

Cocaine people held a different mindset from us. While we still thought of ourselves as spirit-filled hippies trying to be spiritual, they focused on worldly things, which was not where we wanted to be. Nevertheless, as with all things, there are changing circumstances and weakening ideals, and in the end, you still have to eat to live. God forbid any of us should have to get a straight job!

Our Mexican friends persisted in pressing us about smuggling cocaine because the load was lighter than pot. "Hey, *Vato*, you won't have to carry fifteen hundred pounds in an airplane no more," they said. "With cocaine, you can take just six hundred pounds and make the same amount of money, if not more, and with less effort."

We had to admit, it was a pretty solid argument.

As a bunch of peace-loving, spirit-filled hippies, we wanted to deal only with cannabis. However, with Mexico spraying paraquat on all the cannabis crops in their country, we suddenly had nothing to do and no source of income. So, we set aside our principles and snorted some of that devilish white powder. This degradation of our ideals was the beginning of the end.

Eventually, we caved under the pressure and began smuggling blow, which led to the demise of everybody and everything. Coke ruined a lot of lives. It was not a good time for any of us. This was an exceptionally large stone thrown into the lake, a literal boulder.

It was '*COCAINE.*' And it drove us almost to the end of the end.

I consumed kilos of coke, but still, in the words of the immortal Mick Jagger, "Too much is never enough." My nose bled, I couldn't snort, and I stayed clogged up all the time.

So, I started smoking crack, which took a definite toll. It was always party time in those days, and we took *so* many drugs. I was just waking up and getting stoned every day. So long as we were high, we were happy, and that's what it was all about.

I have seen good-hearted human beings, people who grew up with strong moral character and a mindset for goodness. Then, upon taking drugs like cocaine and methamphetamine, they developed a different, primal-based mindset of a neanderthal. I have witnessed that sweet innocent girl next door become a whore and degrade herself with lewd sex of the kind you see only in the darkest, seediest parts of the world.

I, too, became such a casualty to this culture.

While in that lifestyle, I was lying, thieving, and whoring. I became power-hungry and arrogant. But I just didn't care. I had people I thought were my friends, but they proved to be just regular lackeys wanting to get high all the time.

As the old adage says, "If you can remember the Sixties, you weren't there." But I don't recall anything about the Sixties, the Seventies, or the Eighties, and not much about the Nineties for that matter. Eventually, I decided this was not where I wanted to be. So, I left the business and returned to Sulphur Springs.

CHAPTER EIGHTEEN

The Colombia Operation

DC-6 Venture

*"The purpose of the meeting was to discuss
preliminary plans for purchasing
twelve tons of marijuana from Colombia.*

—— **Grand Jury Indictment**

THE CARIBBEAN is a crescent-shaped group of islands more than 2,000 miles long, separating the Gulf of Mexico and the Caribbean Sea to the west and south and the Atlantic Ocean to the east and north. These boundaries include Panama and Central America. By its proximity, the Caribbean forms the most likely transshipment hub port network to serve the United States.

Large vessels known as mainliners transport commercial cargo destined for the United States to a central location outside the U.S. waters. These are then re-parceled into smaller ships known as feeder vessels and distributed throughout U.S. ports.

The 'Caribbean Corridor Strike Force' was an organization that investigated South American-based drug trafficking gangs responsible for the movement of narcotics through the Caribbean.

In conjunction with the War on Drugs, this Strike Force had seriously diminished Colombian traffic through this so-called 'Caribbean Corridor.' This caused the operators in Florida to experience significant problems with their shipments from Colombia, Cuba, and the Everglades.

The Black Tuna Gang was a Miami-based Colombian marijuana-trafficking organization. That was never the official name of the group. Still, the media used it because of the solid gold medallions with a black tuna emblem worn by their members to identify themselves. The Black Tuna Gang was reputed to have imported around one million pounds of marijuana from Colombia into the United States over sixteen months in 1976 and 1977.

Eventually, a joint FBI-DEA effort, known as 'Operation Banco,' brought down the Black Tuna Gang. This gang was so corrupt that during the trial, prosecutors accused certain defendants of attempting to bribe jurors and murder the presiding judge. The court convicted eight members of the gang and gave them significant sentences.

With most of the Black Tuna Gang in prison, the other operators around them began looking for new channels. Buck Cameron met some big-time smugglers with connections in Colombia, and he convinced these players he had all the landing strips they could use. So, we took advantage of this opportunity to become one of those new channels.

So, once again, weed from Colombia was flowing, and a lot of weight was moving. Between this and the paraquat issue, our Mexican imports took a back seat.

Buck Cameron had been a fugitive from Federal authorities since the 1974 Lamesa bust. Nevertheless, in August 1978, he assembled a gathering that included Jay Emerson, Fred Marco, Michael Williams, Phil Conrad, and others at an apartment in Dallas.

The purpose of the meeting was to discuss preliminary plans for purchasing twelve tons of marijuana from Colombia and transporting it by air for distribution in the United States. This project would become known as the 'Colombia Operation.' Five primary components comprised the 'Colombia Operation,' including the 'DC-6 Venture,' the 'Guatemalan Venture,' the 'Oaxacan Transactions,' the 'Jayton Incident,' and the 'Chihuahua Airstrip.'

Subsequent court records would refer to this group from this first set of meetings as the 'DC-6 Venturers.'

The Douglas DC-6 was the last four-engine aircraft before the advent of jets. The plane could fly almost four thousand miles on a single tank of fuel. With the group's approval, Buck Cameron directed Frank Clayton to purchase such a plane for one hundred fifty thousand dollars.

In September 1978, Clayton met with Ben W. Widtfeldt in Long Beach, California, to inspect and discuss acquiring a suitable airplane. In October 1978, Clayton gave Widtfeldt four thousand dollars to secure insurance on the selected aircraft. Two days later, he handed the seller one hundred and fifty thousand dollars in cash to complete the acquisition. Then, he had the DC-6 flown to Santa Maria Airport in San José, Costa Rica, for modification at Cooperativa de Servicios Aero Industries.

A half-dozen members of the DC-6 Venturers gathered at another apartment in Dallas that same month to plan the Colombia Operation further. A subset of this group met several times at the DFW Airport Marina Hotel. The primary purpose of these gatherings was to interview qualified candidates to fly the DC-6 from Colombia to Texas. Buck Cameron, the lone attendee common to all these meetings, offered three hundred and fifty thousand dollars to locate and hire a suitable pilot for the mission. Phil Conrad was acquainted with various pilots, so the group brought him into their confidence to help identify one.

The first pilot prospect rejected the opportunity, saying, "That's how conspiracies start." The second pilot prospect would not participate because he thought the plans were "not together enough" and "the deal would be a bust." Ultimately, they chose Terry Hunter as the pilot because they could find no one else willing to get involved in the scheme.

In December 1978, Buck Cameron and eight others, including Victor Jenkins and Eddie Bandrup, met at a house in Northeast Dallas. The assembly considered a proposal for using Guatemala as a possible refueling site for the Colombia to Texas flight. At one of the meetings, William Winchester showed the attendees one of the three twenty-by-four-foot aluminum ramps he had constructed to facilitate unloading bundles of pot from the aircraft. Over the next few weeks, the meetings continued at the Hunter's Hill Apartments in Dallas and involved even more people in the deal.

CHAPTER NINETEEN

The Colombia Operation

Guatemalan Venture

The group needed a private landing strip
midway between Colombia and Texas.

—— Grand Jury Indictment

IN THE FALL OF **1978**, a separate group formed, which subsequent court records referred to as the 'Guatemalan Venturers.' The group included Americans Victor Jenkins and Eddie Bandrup acting on behalf of the DC-6 Venturers, and Mexican nationals Juan Torres, Alfredo García, and Alphonso Ramirez.

Torres was an attorney who practiced criminal defense law in Mexico City. Unknown to García and Ramirez, he also worked covertly as an informant in cooperation with the U.S. DEA. Additionally, because Torres spoke limited English, he employed Alejandro Lopez as his interpreter. Lopez was also an undercover DEA agent.

The Mexican members of this group had previously planned a scheme to bring pot from the Mexican State of Veracruz into Texas. But, for a variety of reasons, that plan failed to materialize. A few weeks later, this group began planning a new project similar to the DC-6 Venturers' Colombia Operation, albeit smaller in scale. This operation was to import Colombian marijuana using an unspecified but 'large' airplane.

Victor Jenkins told Alphonso Ramirez that he knew some 'Yankees' (DC-6 Venturers) that had a Douglas DC-6 they were planning to fly from Colombia to Texas with a heavy load of marijuana. Ramirez encouraged Jenkins to contact the Yankees to rent the plane from them or become otherwise involved in their venture. However, Jenkins later reported back that the Yankees said they "would have nothing to do with them."

During this period, the Guatemalan Venturers searched aircraft catalogs to find an aircraft appropriate for their venture.

In addition to a suitable airplane, this group needed to find a private landing strip midway between Colombia and Texas. The runway had to be between six- and seven-thousand feet long, capable of supporting a large plane weighing a minimum of ten tons, and suitable for use as a refueling station. This was a common need between the Guatemalan Venturers and the DC-6 Venturers.

Alfredo García contacted attorney Juan Torres, who claimed to have friends in Central America with access to suitable airstrips. In December 1978, Jenkins agreed that García and Ramirez should travel to Guatemala City to meet with Torres and inspect his proposed options.

In Guatemala, Torres' associate, Carlos Villareal, gave them a tour of six potential refueling sites, one of which Ramirez deemed satisfactory. He notified Jenkins that they had located an acceptable airstrip near Flores in an area utilized by oil companies to land DC-6s and DC-7s.

Flores is a town in Guatemala's northern Petén region. It's on an island on Lago Petén Itzá, linked by a causeway to Santa Elena.

Because Victor Jenkins was unwilling to rely upon Ramirez's judgment alone, he sent Eddie Bandrup to approve the clandestine landing strip Carlos Villareal had proposed.

The DC-6 Venturers group owed Alphonso Ramirez for finding the refueling site and securing provisions. Ramirez asked Jenkins for funds to cover the expenses of the inspection tour and the monies owed to Torres for providing his connection to Villareal who had identified the landing strip. Jenkins told him that he would send Bandrup down to deliver two thousand dollars of expense money and inspect the runway to ensure it was sufficient.

Arriving in Guatemala, Bandrup refused to turn over the cash without first inspecting the airstrip for suitability, even despite Ramirez threatening to murder him. He ultimately conveyed the money to Torres before doing the inspection, but he did not give money to Ramirez and forbade Torres to reimburse him directly.

Their inspection revealed that the airstrip was perfect for their purposes, and Bandrup communicated that fact to the DC-6 Venturers in a private telephone conversation.

In December 1978, Jenkins told Ramirez that a lack of financial resources prevented the DC-6 Venturers from making their Colombian trip for at least two to six months.

In early January 1979, Juan Torres contacted Eddie Bandrup through his interpreter, Alejandro Lopez, demanding to meet in Dallas with Bandrup and Jenkins to discuss his compensation for locating the refueling site.

Bandrup and Jenkins arranged to meet Torres and his interpreter. The meeting participants discussed the utilization of the Guatemalan landing strip by the DC-6 Venturers for their Colombia Operation, on which the parties agreed. Jenkins informed Torres that the planned smuggling operation would be two to six months out, placing it in May or June of 1979. It would utilize a large aircraft going through Guatemala, refueling, and continuing to the United States. Torres would be paid fifty percent of his compensation in advance and the balance after accomplishing the refueling mission.

CHAPTER TWENTY

The Colombia Operation

Oaxacan Transactions

"But Victor, the boat sank!"

—— **Alphonso Ramirez**

TO ACCUMULATE ENOUGH MONEY to make the Colombian trip, Victor Jenkins and Alphonso Ramirez planned to execute several 'Oaxacan ('wä-'hä-ken') transactions.'

In early 1979, Jenkins contracted with a supplier of cannabis from the Mexican State of Oaxaca in southern Mexico to purchase eighteen hundred pounds of Oaxacan pot. Ramirez was to transport the load to the Falcon International Reservoir, about nine hundred miles north, where the Rio Grande River flowed through the middle and separated the United States and Mexico.

Ramirez received ten thousand dollars, in addition to reimbursements for costs and expenses, for his efforts in the operation. The estimated profit expected to accrue to Jenkins due to this single transaction was approximately one hundred thousand dollars. Ramirez delivered the contraband to the connection point; unfortunately, the boat transporting the cargo across the Reservoir sank and lost part of the load.

At this time, the connections to the DEA of Torres and Lopez were not known. Accordingly, the question remained unasked as to whether the DEA had sabotaged the boat to cause it to sink.

An attempt at a second Oaxacan transaction proved unsuccessful also. Ramirez had contacted Torres to secure a suitable truck to haul another shipment of marijuana. However, the supplier of the product refused to deal with them because of allegations that Ramircz had brought DEA agents to Oaxaca.

Juan Torres had, in fact, cooperated with the DEA and utilized Alejandro Lopez, a DEA special agent, as his interpreter. The DEA had made plans to arrest the drug traffickers at the Falcon International Reservoir upon their return to the border.

Ramirez could convince neither the suppliers nor Jenkins that he had not taken any DEA agents to Oaxaca. In March 1979, Ramirez arranged a meeting at the LeBaron Hotel in Dallas, including Jenkins, Bandrup, Torres, and his interpreter Alejandro Lopez, to establish his innocence.

Despite numerous attempts by Ramirez to recast the facts of his story, the everchanging tale he wove destroyed any credibility he may have had. All efforts on behalf of Ramirez to exonerate himself failed, so Jenkins and Bandrup excused everyone from the meeting and then had no further contact with any of them.

CHAPTER TWENTY-ONE

The Colombia Operation

Jayton Incident

"Dudes, there ain't no rain out here."

—— **West Texas Locals**

THE AIRCRAFT purchased by the DC-6 Venturers remained in Costa Rica until March 1979. While there, the plane underwent extensive repairs to make it operational and assure its safety and reliability. Additionally, the crew converted it from a passenger to a cargo or freight airplane.

Upon completion of the work, Terry Hunter, Frank Clayton, and others inspected the plane, after which Hunter flew it to Tucson International Airport in Arizona.

During the first five months of 1979, the DC-6 Venturers met almost daily in Dallas.

A DC-6 typically takes a three- to five-man crew – a pilot, co-pilot, flight engineer, navigator, and crewman. The group had already chosen Terry Hunter as the pilot. At the meeting, they selected a co-pilot and certain other people as unloaders of the contraband once the plane arrived. They designated Buck Cameron as the flight engineer and Michael Williams as the crewman for the mission.

The group also discussed potential loading sites in these meetings, including constructing a secluded landing strip near Jayton, Texas, eighty-five miles northwest of Abilene.

In May 1979, Jay Emerson, Michael Williams, and others went to a location near Jayton. There, they used a bulldozer to plow a six-thousand-foot runway big enough to land a DC-6.

The locals in West Texas thought they were building a lake. "Hey, man. There ain't no rain out here!" they shouted. "So, what are y'all plowing, exactly?"

They were plowing an airstrip, of course. But they told the locals, "Oh, yeah, we're gonna make a pond. A big pond."

The locals repeated, shaking their heads, "Dudes, there ain't no rain out here."

Nevertheless, Terry and Jay persevered despite the locals' negativity.

Then, in a foolish move, in May 1979, Michael Williams and a couple of friends made a side deal with some Mexican counterparts. The group used the Jayton airstrip to take a twin-engine airplane to Mexico to bring back some weed. Unfortunately, in the process, they brought the heat down on the strip when they returned. As a result, the police arrested Williams and his friends and seized fifteen hundred pounds of marijuana.

Michael Williams' lawyer, Shawn Carter, was widely regarded as a snake. He was supposed to negotiate an agreement with the DEA for Williams' surrender.

Michael spent the night in Jay's duplex in Carrollton, Texas, and Jay drove him to Carter's office the next day. The plan was for Williams and Carter to walk to the courthouse together.

When Jay arrived home, his phone rang, and it was Michael. Jay said, "How did it go?"

"Well, I'm done for now. I'm ready if you want to come down and pick me up."

"You're ready to leave?"

"Yeah, man. And hurry if you can."

Williams had overheard Carter talking to the prosecutor, making a deal he didn't want. Carter was selling out his client. Michael was pissed. "Some attorney protecting his client."

So, Michael Williams decided to go on the lam.

CHAPTER TWENTY-TWO

The Colombia Operation

Chihuahua Airstrip

As we reached the end of our taxi to the runway,
Michael Williams jumped out of the plane,
yelling, "I'm out of here,"
and took off on foot, running into the distance.

—— **Jay Emerson**

THE AWARENESS of the illegal purpose of the Jayton airstrip on the part of the police negated the group's plan to land the DC-6 there. As an alternative, they decided to utilize a sixty-thousand-acre ranch in a dry lake bed in the northern Mexico State of Chihuahua as a landing strip.

The group had established a definitive route from Colombia to New York City with this new landing strip. The route ran through the ranch in Chihuahua and the Big Bend Ranch State Park in South Texas. Additionally, Buck Cameron had accumulated a small air force to ferry Colombian weed from Chihuahua into Texas for transport to the East Coast.

The group would fly the loads from Colombia to the ranch in Chihuahua in the Douglas DC-6. Then, they would use smaller planes – a Piper Cherokee Six, Cessna, or Aztec – to shuttle loads from Chihuahua across the border into Texas.

For months, the group had kept a ground crew living on the lake bed in Chihuahua. So, Jay, Denny McCarthy, and others went shopping in Dallas and filled grocery carts with non-perishable food and other supplies to support this crew.

In May 1979, Buck Cameron called from a public phone in Richardson, Texas, to a number in Gomez Palacio in the northwest Mexican State of Durango. He asked Terry Hunter to fly the DC-6 to Santa Marta International Airport in the Magdalena Department of Northern Colombia. About two weeks later, Colombian soldiers they had paid would load it with twenty-four thousand pounds of cannabis. Then, Terry would fly the plane to the airstrip in Chihuahua, stopping for fuel at the airstrip in Guatemala that had been arranged with the Guatemalan Venturers.

Buck Cameron also asked Eddie Bandrup and Jay Emerson to fly the Piper Cherokee Six to Chihuahua to bring out the crew of the DC-6. Bandrup and Emerson would also make multiple shuttle trips to transport the Colombian pot from the DC-6 in Chihuahua into Texas.

Phil Conrad and other crew members attempted to fly a rented plane from Love Field in Dallas to the airstrip in Chihuahua to be available as 'unloaders.' However, bad weather prevented them from completing the flight and forced them to return to Love Field. Several days later, they succeeded in making a flight to transport the unloaders to Mexico.

Eddie Bandrup and I drove to the Piper Cherokee Six at Love Field. Our pickup carried open cardboard boxes of food and supplies under a camper shell. The first thing we did was remove the passenger seats from the single-engine plane and store them in the truck.

That same day, we flew the Piper Cherokee Six from Love Field through Fort Stockton, Texas, and to the dry lake bed in Chihuahua, a distance of approximately six hundred forty miles by air. We carried the open cardboard boxes of food and supplies with us.

All the while, a United States Customs airplane covertly trailed behind us.

About forty miles into Mexico, on the way down to land on the airstrip, we detected the U.S. Customs plane following us. I assumed they were profilers and that we fit their profile. However, I was unsure and did not feel good about having them follow us.

Most experienced smuggler pilots would know that when you suspect you have picked up the heat, you execute a specific maneuver to be sure. First, you make a steep right turn, and whoever is following you will match your course. Then you make a sweeping left, and you will be facing each other, and you can see who is after you.

However, being a green pilot, Eddie Bandrup didn't follow the prescribed procedure. Nevertheless, I became more confident about what we were doing because our big aircraft was down there, and the U.S. Customs plane was on the wrong side of the border, so we decided to go on in despite the government plane following us.

We were about fifty miles into Mexico when we started our descent. Through the binoculars, I could see the DC-6 on the landing strip. It was big, a hundred feet long, and over fifty thousand pounds empty.

Eddie and I made a low pass, flying over the DC-6 to let everyone know we had arrived. Then, we made our bank and landed.

Buck had asked us to land on the north end of the lake bed to ensure we had not brought the heat. But we didn't do that; instead, we taxied right up next to the DC-6. When we disembarked, I asked, "How many planes did Buck send today?"

"Just you," one of the unloaders said, looking into the sky.

"Well, who the hell is that flying over us?"

The U.S. Customs plane, a twin-engine Cessna 310, circled overhead.

I imagined the agent thought he was following a Cherokee Six that might be doing a small smuggle. Instead, he flew over a vast sixty-thousand-acre lake bed and saw trucks backed up to an enormous airplane unloading thousands of pounds of marijuana.

The U.S. Customs plane peeled off and climbed rapidly, trying to get enough altitude to signal the authorities, "Hey! There's a DC-6 down there with what appears to be about twenty-five thousand pounds of marijuana!"

After encountering the Cessna, we kicked it into high gear because we had limited time to move all that weight. We mobilized everyone and everything we could to relocate it to various hiding places, including caves in the walls of the dry lake bed of Chihuahua.

After we had unloaded the DC-6, Bandrup and I took off in the Cherokee Six. Terry Hunter took off in the DC-6, and the two airplanes flew a short distance until the DC-6 almost ran out of fuel, so we landed both aircraft. I suggested we open the tanks and burn the big plane to destroy the evidence, but nobody else wanted to do that. We abandoned the DC-6 and everyone climbed into the Cherokee Six.

After a brief time, we all took off again in the Cherokee Six heading towards the United States, piloted by Eddie Bandrup, and carrying five passengers on the return flight, including Buck Cameron, Michael Williams, Terry Hunter, Phil Conrad, and myself.

Along the way, the U.S. Customs plane pulled up beside us. The pilot must have thought we looked like a garbage truck because once we saw him, everyone got out their identification documents, opened a window, and tossed them out.

It was late afternoon by this time, and the cumulonimbus clouds typical of South Texas had built up to a few scattered thunderstorms. We were headed north to the Texas border with the Customs plane beside us. He wanted us to follow him to El Paso, and he was holding a sign in the window with the radio frequency he wanted us to use. We tuned to the station and heard him command us, but we didn't answer.

"Follow me to this airport. Land with me."

He kept threatening us or warning us, I was not sure, "The Mexican air force is on the way, and they will shoot you down. Please follow me to El Paso."

The Customs plane broke off pursuit and headed to El Paso because he ran low on fuel, but we kept going north.

Then, our pilot, Eddie Bandrup, made a bold and daring move to evade radar and capture by any planes coming for us. The pilot decided to fly into a thunderstorm rain shower to avoid further pursuit from the coming air force planes or the Customs plane following us.

The first rain droplets to hit the windscreen sounded like gunshots. Those of us sitting in the back couldn't tell what was happening. We feared at first that the Mexican Air Force was shooting us down.

God Almighty, we're all going to die, I thought.

Remember, there were no seats in this plane, and the turbulent air of the thunderstorm was throwing the aircraft around, and we were bouncing around in the back with nothing to hold onto.

Suddenly, the plane broke out of the clouds and rain into the sunlight. We were not very high above the ground, skirting below the radar. We realized we were not far from Presidio, just across the Rio Grande.

We landed at Presidio Lely International Airport just over the border in Southwest Texas. As soon as we arrived, the Border Patrol showed up because they had been alerted to watch for us at all the airstrips in the area, so we were forced to take off again immediately.

As we reached the end of our taxi to the runway, Michael Williams jumped out of the plane, yelling, "I'm out of here," and took off on foot, running into the distance. The rest of the group stayed aboard and continued home.

We took off again before the authorities could block the runway, but now carrying one fewer passenger.

Because we were low on fuel, we landed at a deserted and unmanned airstrip. At the same time, we were all glad to be back in America, even though we were out of gas in the middle of nowhere. I remembered we had water jugs in the airplane, so I emptied the water and went to fill the jugs with fuel from other planes on the strip, just enough to get us back to Redbird Airport in South Dallas.

Our group maintained an apartment in Dallas as our office and crash pad for guys who came to town to do business. We locals went there every day when we weren't doing anything else. Denny McCarthy was in the office when Michael Williams called.

In his distressed condition, Michael told him what had happened.

"Holy shit!"

Michael said, "I think I can get to El Paso."

"El Paso?! That's about two hundred fifty miles away. How the hell are you gonna do that?"

"I dunno, I'll figure it out."

"Okay. I'll get down there somehow and meet you."

Apparently, Michael had Scotty 'beam him up,' to get to El Paso. Either that, or he caught a friendly long-haul trucker who just happened to be on his way to El Paso and was happy to accommodate him.

Denny took a Southwest Airlines flight from Love Field to El Paso, where he rented a car and met Michael. Then, they drove back to Fort Worth together.

CHAPTER TWENTY-THREE

The Colombia Operation

Paying the Piper

"The Mexican Police wrapped him in a tarp,
sprayed mineral water mixed with jalapeño juice up his nose,
and then left him to bake in the sun."

—— **Jay Emerson**

AFTER OUR ABANDONMENT of the DC-6, it took two more weeks for the Mexican Police to get to the site, and they came in the middle of the night. Upon arrival, the officers awakened the local townspeople, assembled them in the square, and began grilling them. "So, who are these guys, and where are they? And where is their contraband?"

Then, the Mexican Police proceeded to beat certain high profile individuals from the townspeople to get them to disclose the location of the hidden cannabis. Consequently, because of the severity of the beatings, the selected townspeople relented and told the Police about the caves.

The Mexican Authorities rounded up the son of the man who owned the sixty-thousand-acre ranch in Chihuahua, from where the DC-6 had taken off. The Mexican Police wrapped the son in a tarp, sprayed mineral water mixed with jalapeño juice up his nose, and then left him to bake in the sun. Such an excruciating torture treatment drove the son's father to rat out Buck Cameron and Aaron Stanton.

Only a few days after we landed in June 1979, from information provided by the townspeople and their own aerial surveillance, the Mexican authorities discovered the abandoned DC-6 near Ocampo in the Mexican State of Coahuila on a dry lake bed named 'Milk Lake.' They found eleven pounds of marijuana debris and seeds inside the plane, which was low on fuel and otherwise empty.

The Mexican Police uncovered a portion of the twelve-ton cache of Colombian marijuana in caves on a farm called Rancho El Guaje. That was near another dry lake bed named 'King's Chemist,' a short distance north of where the authorities had discovered the abandoned airplane. Also found at the site were numerous opened cardboard boxes containing supplies and food. Once the Feds located the DC-6, they could determine our flight path from the plane's flight data recorder in the black box. They knew where we had gone and what we were doing. Their only problem was that they couldn't identify all the involved parties.

The DC-6 Venturers had met at an apartment in North Dallas a month earlier to discuss establishing a plan for transporting the remaining pot from Mexico to Texas.

Buck Cameron and Michael Williams were still fugitives from Federal authorities then.

Phil Conrad received twenty-five hundred dollars to procure a shuttle aircraft. He used these funds and an additional five thousand dollars as a down payment on the 'lease-purchase' of a small Aero Grand Commander.

Because Terry Hunter refused to pilot the Commander, we offered Blackie Zielinski the shuttle job despite our concerns about his qualifications. He had a tendency to fly 'outside the lines,' pushing the aircraft too hard, making dangerous maneuvers, putting the aircraft and its passengers at risk. Hunter later agreed to fly the Commander to Arlington Municipal Airport from Love Field, where Conrad had delivered it after its acquisition in Florida.

Blackie Zielinski soon confirmed the group's reservations about his skillset by damaging the plane while over-boosting its engines on a practice flight. So, we never utilized the Grand Commander as a shuttle airplane for the venture. However, we flew at least one other aircraft, a twin-engine Navajo, to perform transport services between northern Mexico and the United States.

Phil Conrad received one hundred pounds of Colombian weed to do a side deal on his own. In July, he made a partial payment to Buck Cameron of fifteen thousand dollars cash on the product's purchase price. Witnessing the transaction, Jenkins held up to the light one of the hundred-dollar bills and remarked, "DEA."

Unfortunately, we later discovered that Conrad had worn a wire to the meeting and had implicated everyone involved. We presumed the DEA may have busted him and incentivized him to roll over in return for a better deal.

Over time, things changed. The dozen or so of the original group planning this deal became a more loose-knit connection. We no longer hung out together very much. It had become more of a business than a friendship.

We retained some of our original principles, but mainly, we just wanted to make money and get high. We had essentially lost our primary intent to bring pot to the world to liberate the minds of humanity. The drugs were now more important than the fundamental spiritual purpose. I knew it then but did not want to admit it.

Maybe this was just part of the natural process of growing up.

<<<>>>

Over the next two years, the DEA issued indictments for sixteen people, including Buck Cameron and Aaron Stanton for the Colombia Operation.

At that time, Cameron had already started putting together another DC-6 deal. But DEA Agent in Charge Dean Gates got to Buck's wife, Susan, and scared her into demanding that Buck turn himself in. So, he finally relented and reported to prison for the first time.

Still, the DEA did not know that William Winchester and I were involved, so we were not yet indicted.

However, in March 1980, the DEA filed an indictment in the Northern District of Texas, Dallas Division. It charged eighteen people, including Buck Cameron, Fred Marco, Victor Jenkins, Terry Hunter, Eddie Bandrup, William Winchester, and me. The charges ranged from conspiring to import and distribute imported marijuana to possessing and intending to distribute contraband.

Phil Conrad, an unindicted co-conspirator, was a key government witness who testified concerning the roles performed by different conspirators in return for a grant of immunity. He had attended most of the meetings relating to the Colombia Operation.

A jury trial of just Bandrup, Jenkins, Hunter, and Marco returned guilty verdicts for all. The other indictees had previously entered guilty pleas, had their charges dismissed, or had evaded apprehension.

The court denied motions for new trials by each of the four defendants, so all appealed. In January 1981, the judge imposed prison sentences: Victor Jenkins – five years, Eddie Bandrup and Terry Hunter – four years, and Fred Marco – three years. The Board of Parole would determine parole eligibility. In June 1982, the Appeals Court heard the arguments and affirmed all the convictions.

My indictment came down in March 1980. I said goodbye to my mother and went on the lam again with Kim and our son, Jeremy. However, I could not flee the country because INTERPOL was looking for me since my crimes had crossed international borders.

Jeremy was six, and Kim and I wanted to put him in school. Unfortunately, that would require us to present our social security numbers, thereby exposing our identities and location. We also needed jobs to feed ourselves and provide a roof over our heads. Both imposed similar requirements and risks.

I was a vegetarian then but could not maintain that practice because of our circumstances. Living on the Guadalupe River in San Marcos, Texas, I went down to the river's edge, caught a couple of crawfish, and ate them. And my son looked at me and said, "Yeah, Dad, you're some vegetarian." Even my son was losing respect for me. After being on the run for over three years, we realized the situation was not working for us. We had no more pot coming in and were broke and starving.

Finally, I called my mother for help and said, "Listen, Mama, I'm going to turn myself in. You have a grandbaby here, and I know you've wanted to see him. I know you don't think much of Kim; not many people do. But would you consider taking in my baby and his mother for a time?" Being a devoted mother, she agreed to care for them while I was in prison.

William Winchester and I negotiated deals with the DEA to surrender in return for reduced sentences. So, William went first. Then I turned myself in to the Dallas Marshall and pleaded guilty to possessing twelve tons of marijuana with intent to distribute. The court sentenced me to eighteen months in Federal Correctional Institution Seagoville.

After this first conviction, I divorced Kim because I thought it would not work out with me being in prison and Jeremy and her being on the outside. I felt terrible about this because Kim had put up with all my bullshit for seven years. I have to give her credit, though; she did a damn good job raising my son, a really great job. But to be perfectly frank, I didn't love her enough to stay married.

CHAPTER TWENTY-FOUR

The Ruidoso Operation

"Yeah, 'just one more deal.' Ain't it always?"

—— **Jay Emerson**

THE EIGHTEEN MONTHS OF IMPRISONMENT I endured for my first conviction apparently did not cause me enough suffering to convince me to change my ways. As a result, when I left the Seagoville Satellite Camp, I had no more sense than when I went in.

So, I started the whole cycle over, recommencing my heavy drug involvement, including smoking crack and smuggling cocaine. Buck Cameron, Aaron Stanton, and I worked out of Oaxaca and Michoacán, getting some beautiful marijuana out of the interior of Mexico.

Aaron later met his demise in Mexico when his bodyguard assassinated him with a bullet to the back of his head.

At a certain point, I became so burned out that I gave it up.

Not having seen my mother for about a year, I showed up at her house one day with my suitcase and my addictions. She was struggling with cancer then, so I paid the bills for her and took care of the family responsibilities.

Of course, my mother knew what I had been up to the whole time. It's funny how mothers know these things.

That's when I decided to dry out. My mother owned a twenty-six-acre pond on her property in East Texas. So, for thirty days, I sat in a little boat all day and never caught a single fish.

I thought and thought until I figured everything out. Then, I never did cocaine again.

Instead, I went through a severe state of depression. My ex-wife Kim refused to allow me to see my son because she considered me an idiot. The feeling was mutual. I suspected she just wanted to use him as a pawn to get more child support.

I started a landscaping business, doing yard maintenance, which was easy for me. The overhead and entry fees were both minimal – only six hundred dollars. So, I bought a mower, a blower, and a weed eater and loaded everything into the bed of my El Camino.

Since the family business involved funerals, we knew the cemetery board members responsible for hiring groundskeepers. So, I started mowing cemeteries as my first customer, which worked well. It was very simple work, and I never had a complaint.

Escaping the old world was essential to me. Isolating myself from everybody connected with that life was critical. I could not hang with those people and stay straight.

Nevertheless, one day, Cousin Buck, the 'Domineering Master Manipulator,' showed up intending to talk me into doing 'just one more deal.'

Yeah, 'just one more deal.' Ain't it always?

"Hey, man!" he said. "I have a line on fifteen hundred pounds of weed! Plus, I have the pilot and the plane, which will fly everything back to Ruidoso, New Mexico. I don't know anybody else who can do this. I don't trust anyone else, and I'm not gonna leave this stuff to someone else."

Buck had already been under investigation by the DEA for months. Besides that, the pilot was Terry Hunter, who flew the DC-

6 used in the Colombia operation. In the meantime, the police had busted Hunter in a twin-engine airplane carrying six hundred pounds of cocaine as part of another deal. So, of course, he ratted out his partners in that deal like a big boy to keep himself out of jail.

"Okay," I said, "What the hell? I'll do it." Yes, I know. Sometimes, I can be a very foolish man.

Buck had run into Hunter recently and brought him in to pilot the plane for the Ruidoso Operation.

He also had made an arrangement with the plane's owner for the use of his plane, for which the owner wanted ten ounces of cocaine in return. That equated to twenty thousand dollars. If the aircraft went down or got lost, the owner would call his insurance company and say someone stole his airplane. He would come out with his original investment plus the insurance proceeds.

So, we needed to come up with some coke. No problem. We could do that.

Unfortunately, as a newly minted DEA informant, Terry Hunter ratted us out, and the DEA was waiting for us when we landed in Ruidoso with the ten ounces of cocaine.

In November 1987, the court charged us with trafficking a controlled substance with intent to distribute. In September 1988, we pleaded guilty to the charges. The judge gave me nine years at the Penitentiary of New Mexico, a men's maximum-security state prison about fourteen miles south of Santa Fe. Then he graciously suspended six years of that sentence, leaving me three years to serve. My lawyer and I decided to appeal the verdict. I would be out on bond for another year or two before I had to report to prison were we to lose the appeal.

In the meantime, I intensified my training in martial arts, which I had started when I was sixteen, trying to emulate my Cousin Buck. I went to Reno, Nevada, fought semi-full contact, and won the United States National Championship in my bracket. I was ranked in the top ten in the United States by the American Taekwondo Association. I traveled as far east as Atlanta, Georgia, and as far west as Reno, Nevada, every month or so to train or fight.

In 1989, I got a call telling me to report to the Penitentiary of New Mexico in two weeks.

CHAPTER TWENTY-FIVE

The Memphis Operation

Temptation

"Hell, yeah, we can do that. Bring us five."

—— **Buck Cameron**

ALMOST IMMEDIATELY, my cousin Buck showed up again, saying, "Hey, man, check this out. My connections in Juarez have fifty thousand pounds of weed already across the border in El Paso, and we can have all of it we want."

Ooohhh, noo! Not again. It could not be possible he was telling me about yet another, 'Just one more deal.' Christ! In two weeks, I had to report to prison in New Mexico for the last 'Just one more deal.'

Of course, with Buck being the relentlessly manipulative devil he was, it wasn't long before I caved. After all, his logic was sound, if not misguided.

"Well, I can't say as I'm looking forward to returning to jail any time soon."

"Hey, I feel you, brother."

"Anyway, what the hell are they gonna do if I go on the lam? Tack on another year?"

He did not answer my rhetorical question but shrugged his shoulders as if he didn't understand. He did, but he was a good enough salesman to know to stop talking once his customer nodded his head 'Yes.'

So, I skipped out. Again.

Fifty thousand pounds of marijuana represented significant money. So, I decided to take the risk. If things went wrong, I could go to my lawyer, turn myself in, and serve my time.

At least I would have all the money I needed when I got out. Hell, I might even be happy. This sounded like a good idea to me. So, I let rip one of my loud one-note laughs as I often did, "HA!" And that sealed the deal.

Buck's Juarez connections transported twelve and a half tons of marijuana in about nine hundred fifty-five-gallon drums and delivered them to El Paso for storage in a warehouse. The Mexican factories put a border stamp on the eighteen-wheelers, which allowed them to be waved right on through the entry ports and into the United States.

This was some of the most beautiful pot I had seen in three years. You could buy grass for about two hundred bucks a pound and sell it in New York for a thousand bucks a pound. Do the math. Fifty million dollars at retail and a forty-million-dollar profit! Hoo-wee!

Besides waiting to go to jail, no one in our group had anything else going on at the time, and nobody wanted to do anything. All of a sudden, here came Buck's Juarez connection offering to provide us with five hundred pounds. "*Hola, Vatos!* Y'all do five?"

"Hell, yeah, we can do that," Buck said, "Bring us five."

Our crew for this operation, consisting of Buck Cameron, Bernie Rémy, Carl Cochran, and I, took five hundred pounds of marijuana to grease the markets the first time. So, I drove the load up to Virginia Beach and New York by myself and returned with the money in two weeks.

We sat for two more weeks until the guy called again and said, "How about five more?"

Considering the first delivery worked out so well, Buck said, "Yeah, get us five more." Of course, the idiot brought not five *hundred* but five *thousand* pounds of weed in an eighteen-wheeler!

Ha! We were no more prepared to handle five thousand pounds of pot than we were to land a man on the moon. But no one wanted to let it go back, so Buck said, "Oh, hell yeah, we can do this!"

Soon, Buck Cameron, Bernie Rémy, Carl Cochran, and I met in a Dallas motel with an eighteen-wheeler chock-full of fifty-five-gallon drums filled with marijuana.

The first thing we needed was a place to unload everything. So, we packed it all into a large U-Haul truck and ran it out to Victor Jenkin's house about sixty miles east in Canton, Texas. Victor bought a thousand pounds. With the proceeds from that sale, we had enough money to figure out what to do with the remaining four thousand pounds. Buck said, "Well, I guess we better line up some stash houses and cars to start running this stuff up to New York."

Everyone agreed we needed to get it out of there. Two weeks later, we rented a Ryder truck and loaded it. Two thousand pounds would go to Virginia Beach and another two thousand to New York in thousand dollars-a-pound lots. So, if you're good at arithmetic or have a calculator, you'll see that would be worth four million dollars!

"Tell you what, I will drive it," I said. "Wherever you want it to go. But you gotta pay me in product at cost, not retail. At cost only so I can sell it, and then I'm gonna get out. I plan to open a self-defense school near Pepperdine University for all those young nubile nymphets who can't defend themselves."

This was the dream I had been chasing for many years. It would be my way back to legitimacy.

CHAPTER TWENTY-SIX

The Memphis Operation

Interdiction

"Oh, yes, please, Officer.
Some help moving these four thousand pounds
of marijuana out of this truck
and into that other one would be great.
Thank you for offering. That's very kind of you."

—— **Jay Emerson**

IN THE LATE EIGHTIES, the Drug Enforcement Agency was aware of smugglers bringing massive quantities of drugs from Mexico into Texas and transporting them to other states. Part of the DEA's drug interdiction practices was to have law enforcement officers in the states surrounding Texas profile vehicles with Texas license plates as potential smugglers.

The DEA pulled many of those vehicles over for alleged traffic violations, real or imagined. Even if you were Grandma and Grandpa in an RV, they might pull you over just for having Texas plates.

Thank God, the rental truck I was driving with four thousand pounds of marijuana in the back had Indiana plates. So, I said to Buck, Bernie, and Carl, who would be following in two other vehicles, "Y'all have Texas plates on your cars. So, once we're on the road, I don't want either of you coming anywhere near me."

"Well, we want to watch what's happening," Bernie Rémy whined. Understandably, he was the money man on this deal and had put down two hundred thousand dollars on the load.

So, I said, "Well, I'll tell you what's gonna happen. If anything breaks down on this truck, I'm gonna pull off to the side of the road, climb out, and walk away."

"What? Why?" Rémy asked.

"Well, what would you have me do? Stand there until the cops come to rescue me?"

"Well, we might rent another truck."

"Yeah. Rent another truck and then try to switch all this stuff on the side of the interstate," I said. "Come on, man! In no time, a Highway Patrol Officer would drive up on us and ask if we needed any help."

In a sarcastic tone, I berated Bernie, "Oh, yes, please, Officer. Some help moving these four thousand pounds of marijuana out of this truck and into that other one would be great. Thank you for offering. That's very kind of you."

Embarrassed, Bernie said, "Yeah. Well, we're going to follow you anyway."

"Whatever, just stay many miles behind me."

Bernie and Carl would follow in a white Mercedes-Benz with tinted windows, and Buck would follow in a Chrysler New Yorker. We expected to leave the truck in New York after we delivered the pot. Each of us would help unload the product, Buck would drive me back home, and Bernie had put up the money for this gig.

On January 11, 1989, our convoy left Dallas, driving northeast up Interstate 30 until we reached Little Rock and then took Interstate 40 east through Arkansas to Memphis, Tennessee.

On a misty, rainy day around lunchtime, we crossed the Mississippi River on the Hernando de Soto Bridge into Memphis. What a beautiful place that was – the river, the bridge, the city in the near distance. Traffic was building up and slowing as we neared Danny Thomas Boulevard near the St. Jude Children's Research Hospital. Soon, it came to a complete halt.

My two friends, Bernie Rémy and Carl Cochran, followed me in the Mercedes two or three miles behind. Buck Cameron followed a distance behind them in the Chrysler. Buck had brought two girlfriends with him, neither of whom had ever been out of Hopkins County. He planned to take them to New York to show them a good time. As the adapted version of the old saying goes, you can take the girl out of the [county], but you can't take the [county] out of the girl.

Despite being in heavy traffic, I did not worry about anyone making a connection between our three vehicles. The truck would blend in with everyone else. Of course, just then, my Yahoo friends in the Mercedes with the Texas plates pulled up right behind me as I sat stopped in traffic. *Sonovabitch!*

With the vehicles passing through Danny Thomas Boulevard, Detective R.G. Coleman, an off-duty Memphis Police officer, focused on two vehicles driving eastbound on Interstate 40 and approaching the interchange at Canada Road near Lakeland.

A white Mercedes-Benz with Texas license plates appeared to follow a Ryder rental truck with an Indiana license plate. Detective Coleman became suspicious that the vehicles may be riding in tandem and decided to follow them on the interstate.

Trailing the two vehicles, Detective Coleman realized that a third vehicle, a Chrysler New Yorker also with Texas license plates, appeared to be riding in the convoy. Coleman noticed that the Mercedes and the Chrysler followed the truck's path every time it changed lanes.

I spotted a truck stop about twenty-five miles out of Memphis near Lakeland. My stomach told me it was lunchtime, and I was hungry, so I pulled into the truck stop's parking lot. Memphis was known as the barbeque capital of the world, and I had my heart set on having some Memphis-style dry ribs.

Bernie and Carl pulled up behind me as soon as I stopped. Buck, with his girlfriends in the Chrysler, stopped behind them, and everyone got out of the vehicles and gathered behind the truck to talk.

Buck charged at Bernie and lit into him with both feet, "What the hell are you thinking, man?" Buck said shoving Bernie in the chest with both hands. "Thought I told you. Stay *far* behind Jay! Get off his ass, or you're gonna get us all busted." Buck shoved him again. "Now, back off, dumbass!"

"Yeah, yeah, okay, Buck, I understand," Bernie said, "Sorry, man. Relax."

To my chagrin, the restaurant was closed, so I said, "Alright, let's go on down the road a ways and find another place to eat. I got a hankerin' for some barbeque."

Detective Coleman called his office at the Memphis Police Department to request backup assistance. Coleman followed as all three vehicles pulled off the interstate at the Canada Road exit into the truck stop parking lot. He parked at a discreet vantage point and observed the occupants talking together.

Lieutenant Larry Clemmer, also from the Memphis Police Department, joined Detective Coleman in his unmarked police cruiser. In the meantime, another one of Coleman's supervisors notified the Tennessee Highway Patrol about his suspicions. However, the supervisor did not take note of the speeding or improper operation of any of the three vehicles.

Everyone in our group climbed back into our vehicles and headed out. The drizzling rain had made the road slick, and I got trapped in the left lane, trying to pass people in the right lane to get over. *Why wouldn't they move over? Those bastards just speed up and won't let me by.*

The speed limit was fifty-five mph, so I gave up and slowed a little.

With the three vehicles preparing to reenter the interstate, heading east from Memphis toward Nashville, Lieutenant Clemmer took a position ahead of the convoy, and Detective Coleman followed behind. Lieutenant Clemmer clocked the Mercedes-Benz and the truck going seventy-two mph in a fifty-five-mph zone. Clemmer notified the Tennessee Highway Patrol dispatcher that Memphis Police Department officers were following three vehicles eastbound on I-40 and that two were speeding.

Officers of the Highway Patrol caught up with the convoy in a short while. Sergeant Allen Cathy of the Highway Patrol observed the truck weaving on the road. So, he stopped the truck driven by Jay Emerson after noticing its erratic operation.

CHAPTER TWENTY-SEVEN

The Memphis Operation

Detention and Arrest

"Oh, man, I guess I could run off across this field,
but I don't know where I am.
So, there's no chance in hell
that's gonna work out well."

—— **Jay Emerson**

"WELL, SHIT! THIS COULD GET MESSY," I mumbled, grabbing my paperwork, including my road log and my inventory of contents. Exiting the truck, I walked to the back, where Sergeant Allen Cathy stood. *Everything should be all right, I thought. By all appearances, I look like I am supposed to be driving this truck. My story will be that I'm going to New York to start a new job.* "Yes, Sir? What seems to be the problem, Officer?"

"This is a fifty-five-mph zone, Sir, and I clocked you at seventy-two."

I didn't think I was speeding, but I knew he just needed a reason to pull me over so he would have something to put in his report. So, I didn't argue.

When Sergeant Cathy watched Jay Emerson exit the cab and carry his paperwork to the back of the truck, it appeared to him that Emerson was intoxicated.

Upon investigation, Sergeant Cathy also discovered that Emerson had two prior felony drug convictions and was out on an appeal bond for the second. So, he arrested Emerson for driving while intoxicated. Later, Cathy learned that this truck was involved in the speeding incident reported by Detective Coleman.

At about the same time, Patrolman Ross stopped the Mercedes, driven by Bernie Rémy and occupied by Carl Cochran.

Ross had stopped the Mercedes about one hundred yards behind the Ryder truck. Then the Officer moved the Mercedes off the road and closer to the truck for safety reasons since it was raining.

Patrolman Ross had not witnessed the vehicle speeding but still issued a speeding ticket to Rémy. He did not release either of the men at that time.

Soon after the stopping of the Ryder truck by Sergeant Cathy, Lieutenant Clemmer arrived and detected a strong scent of marijuana emanating from the truck. The other officers recognized the slightly weedy, piney, 'skunk' scent that suggested marijuana.

The officers detained Rémy and then informed him that they were conducting a drug investigation.

After the officers at the scene sensed marijuana in the truck, they asked Bernie Rémy, the owner of the Mercedes, for permission to search his vehicle. Bernie gave the officers his written consent to do so.

The officers found marijuana and other incriminating evidence in their search of the Mercedes. So, they arrested Rémy and Cochran for possession.

The officers also stopped the Chrysler, driven by Buck Cameron and occupied by two females, Trish Ingraham and Sally Simone. Searching the vehicle, the officers found other material evidence. However, the court would later suppress this evidence at trial. The officers also learned that Cameron was Emerson's first cousin, so they arrested Buck Cameron for possession.

At that point, I realized we were busted. While standing at the back of the truck with the officer, all the blood suddenly rushed out of my head, and I collapsed down to one knee. By instinct, I braced myself with one hand on the ground, feeling as if I was going to pass out. Realizing I better stand up, or the officer might think something was weird, I shakily stood up but immediately fell back to the ground.

The officer must have thought I was having a heart attack. Sergeant Cathy helped me to my feet and sat me on the truck's rear bumper. As I sat there, my mind said, *Oh, my God! Oh, my God! Oh, my God! I'm out on a bail bond. This is it! This is it!*

Sergeant Cathy appeared to be quite concerned about me. "Are you alright, Sir?"

Cathy was unaware of what was happening or what was in the back of the truck. He only knew he was supposed to pull this truck over, and now, he thought its driver might be having a heart attack.

"Oh, man, I guess I could run off across this field, but I don't know where I am. So, there's no chance in hell that's gonna work out well."

"Sir, may we look in the back of the truck?" Sergeant Cathy asked.

"No, not without a search warrant," I said.

Cathy cuffed me, moved me to the back of his cruiser, and went to obtain a search warrant.

Lieutenant Clemmer requested a drug-sniffing dog and a search warrant for the truck. With the dog being fifty miles away in

Memphis, it took almost an hour and a half for the animal to arrive. Upon arrival, the dog went right to work and soon sat down, indicating the presence of drugs in the truck.

"Well, what did the dog do?" I asked.

"The dog sat."

"Every dog sits. That dog is not growling or scratching."

"Well, this dog just sits, which means he's got it."

Searching the truck, officers found a lease agreement in the passenger compartment. They discovered what they were looking for after opening the truck's rear door.

Chapter Twenty-Eight

The Memphis Operation

Strike Three! You're Out!

"Mister Emerson, you and Mister Cameron
will be classified as 'career criminals'
since this will be the third felony conviction
for each of you, so y'all are each looking at
thirty years and maybe even life."

—— **Lieutenant Larry Clemmer**

THIS WAS THE LARGEST MARIJUANA BUST in Tennessee history at that time. So, we made *Good Morning America* for three days straight and the local news three times a day for seven days. I probably even got some politicians elected on this platform. "This will not stand! This cannot be in our state!" these fat old politicians would shout as they pointed their greasy fingers at me.

That was it. That was it.

After the arrests, the police impounded all three vehicles and took everyone to the precinct office in downtown Memphis.

The police deposited Buck Cameron, Carl Cochran, Bernie Rémy, Trish Ingraham, Sally Simone, and me in separate interrogation rooms.

My thoughts spun as I sat alone at a table. *Mom's going to be so disappointed. Of course, I jumped bail on my Ruidoso conviction when I faced only three years on that. So, what are they going to do to me now?*

After a substantial wait, Lieutenant Clemmer entered the room and sat at the table opposite me. He stared at me for some time without speaking. Finally, "Mister Emerson, in March 1980, you pleaded guilty to conspiring to import and distribute imported marijuana and possessing the contraband with intent to distribute. The court sentenced you to eighteen months in Federal Correctional Institution Seagoville."

"Strike one!" The Lieutenant said, holding up his right index finger.

"In September 1988, you pleaded guilty to possessing ten ounces of cocaine. The court sentenced you to nine years at the Penitentiary of New Mexico, with six years suspended. After appealing the case, you skipped out while on an appeal bond. At the time, the court had scheduled you to report to prison only two weeks later."

"Strike two!" Clemmer said, holding up two fingers.

"Now, we have caught you with four thousand, four hundred, fifty-seven pounds of marijuana in a Ryder rental truck on the way to New York. It will be strike three for you if we convict you for that. Are you aware of what happens when you have three strikes?"

"I strike out?"

"Well, I guess you might say that, but with three felony drug convictions, you could be looking at thirty years."

Looking at the Officer, I said, "Thirty what?!"

"Thirty years," he said. "Oh, yeah, didn't you hear? About eight months ago, President Reagan enacted these mandatory minimums, and the way I see it, you're looking at about thirty years."

"My God! Why didn't anybody tell us this?" Stunned, I said, "I guarantee you; eighty percent of the smuggler's market would've dropped out if you had only told people what they were dealing with."

"Well, Sir, you'll be looking at thirty years as a three-time convicted felon." He paused to let that sink in. "Do you want to try to help yourself?"

Hanging my head, I stared at the floor. *Thirty years?!*

"So, who are you, and who are these yahoos you're with?"

Again, shaking my head, I stared at the floor, oblivious to what Clemmer said. No way can it be thirty years. This was all I could think about.

"Listen. Those DEA bastards don't really care about where the dope came from or where it was going. DEA just wants to know who you four yahoos are because y'all appear to be somebody."

No answer.

"Four thousand, four hundred, fifty-seven pounds of marijuana. That's unheard of in this state."

Pregnant pause.

"Tell you what," Clemmer said, "if y'all cooperate with us on what the four of you were doing, we'll cut you a deal. The mandatory minimum will be ten years for Cochran and Rémy because this is their first bust. "Mister Emerson, you and Mister Cameron will be classified as 'career criminals' since this will be the third felony conviction for each of you. So y'all are each looking at thirty years and maybe even life."

Eventually, the police brought Cameron, Cochran, Rémy, and me together in one room and left us alone. That seemed a strange and suspicious action to all of us.

Carl said, "Look y'all, Buck and Jay are looking at thirty years or more. Bernie and I are looking at only ten years." Carl looked at Bernie as if seeking his agreement. "So, if it would help y'all to receive a reduced sentence, you have our permission to rat us out."

"No," Buck said. "Let's fight this. Let's fight this. The cops don't know what they have. None of us can say anything so we can fight this. The cops have to prove that I knew something."

Buck looked around the room and then said, "That would require everyone to stay quiet. Nobody can say anything."

Buck looked at me and said, "When I'm out, I'll come for you because I got all this money in my stock. Jay, I'll sell our company, the furniture store and funeral home. I'll sell my stock, and I'll rescue you."

The police separated our group again, after they had watched and listened through a one-way mirror. Now, they understood what we were and were not willing to do.

Stewing on that for a minute, I realized the DEA had me cold. There was no way I could escape this one. I was leaning toward pleading guilty but was not ready to tell anyone.

Lieutenant Clemmer entered the room and said, "I must tell you, your cousin, Mister Cameron, decided to fight this; consequently, he may be facing life in prison."

"Yeah, I figured as much. That does not come as a surprise."

"Mister Emerson, with a conviction on this charge, you will be a three-strike career criminal. The government will also charge you under the RICO Act for organized crime."

"The RICO Act? What the hell is that?"

"The RICO Act is part of the Organized Crime Control Act of 1970. The Racketeer Influenced and Corrupt Organizations Act (RICO) makes it unlawful to acquire, operate, or receive income from an enterprise through a pattern of racketeering activity."

Clemmer paused to let that sink in.

"Mister Emerson, you've been doing this all your life. So, if you plead guilty and save the taxpayers' money and the government's time, we'll ensure you receive the bottom end of the sentencing guidelines."

Jay said, "All right. What's that?"

"Twenty-five years."

Oh, shit! Twenty-five years? Fuck me! "And what if I don't?"

"Well, if you don't and if you lose, we will enhance your sentence, and you will get life imprisonment with no parole. I guarantee you will never see daylight again. With twenty-five years, at least, you'll get out. After serving about twenty-one years, you'll be less than sixty when you're out, and you'll be alive. Perhaps you can still do something with your life."

Slowly looking around the room, I considered my options. Realizing I had none, I said, "Okay, I'll plead guilty."

Buck went to court to try to beat the rap. He tried to beat the sighting of the Mercedes traveling along with the truck driven by Emerson.

In the meantime, the police threatened to take away the children of his two girlfriends who had been with him in the Chrysler, so they caved right away and ratted him out. All they had to do was convince the court beyond the shadow of a doubt that Buck was involved.

Trish Ingraham, the owner of the Chrysler and a passenger on the trip, testified that Cameron offered her a thousand dollars to use her car. The purported purpose was to help Jay Emerson move furniture to New York and then drive him back home.

Trish Ingraham also testified that, instead of meeting Emerson in Sulphur Springs, they detoured one hundred sixty miles to Dallas, where Emerson had already loaded the truck with marijuana.

Cameron also rented a room in Dallas that he had never used, and he and his passengers stayed at a motel separate from the truck in Texarkana, Arkansas.

Ingraham's niece, Sally Simone, was Cameron's friend and another passenger in the Chrysler. Sally knew Carl Cochran only through her association with Cameron. Seeing the Mercedes traveling with them, Simone asked Cameron about it, and he told her to mind her own business.

The jury found Buck Cameron, Carl Cochran, and Bernie Rémy guilty. The court sentenced Cochran and Rémy to one hundred twenty-one months imprisonment, five years of supervised release, and a twenty-five thousand dollar fine. The court sentenced Cameron to life imprisonment without parole.

For my guilty plea, my sentence was twenty-five years imprisonment. Two hundred ninety-two months, to be more precise, followed by ten years of supervised release and a twenty-five thousand-dollar fine.

The prosecution returned to all our priors and deemed us an organized crime unit. A task force in Dallas laid out a pyramid diagram of the organization. They could see the whole organization, so they pulled in another drug family when they busted us.

The task force assumed that Richard Trout also had to be involved if Buck Cameron was involved, though we had not seen Richard for years. Richard Trout was one of Buck Cameron's brothers-in-law. Richard got heat on him because he got busted and blamed us. On the day of Cameron's, Cochran's, and Rémy's convictions, Richard Trout was in another room preparing to testify against them.

From that point, I never saw the light of day until twelve years later.

Act Three

DOING THE TIME

CHAPTER TWENTY-NINE

<u>Diagnostics</u> [5]

The culture in maximum security prisons
is more akin to a war zone than a correctional facility.
Inmates often don't engage in rational thought.
They think in terms of power, fear, and coercion.

—— **BOP Security Levels Guidance**

THE PRISON SECURITY LEVEL is the most critical determinant of an inmate's quality of life. The Federal Bureau of Prisons (BOP) calculates a Security Point Total score using a classification system. This score is a significant component in determining the inmate's security level of incarceration.

The Designation and Sentence Computation Center (DSCC) is the stand-alone BOP office that calculates inmate sentences and determines prison assignments. DSCC staff consider various factors when classifying BOP inmates.

These factors include inmate-specific information (e.g., history of violence, age, sentence length, medical needs, and others) and Bureau-specific information (e.g., prison population considerations, specific security issues, etc.)

Vulnerable populations include sex offenders, informants (aka, 'Rats'), and homosexuals. Extreme violence creates an unsafe prison environment for these vulnerable people. Inmates with a history of cooperation with the government or sex offenses cannot safely remain in the general population.

DSCC bases its prison security level determinations on documentation from the U.S. Marshals Service and the U.S.

Probation Department. These documents include the Pre-Sentence Report, Judgment and Commitment Order, and Statement of Reasons. DSCC officials use these so-called 'Diagnostic' documents to classify inmates to prison security levels and specific prisons.

DSCC considers many factors when making initial designation determinations, including prison security level indication, inmate supervision, and physical and mental health care needs. They also consider the available bed space, proximity to the inmate's home residence, judicial recommendations, separation orders between inmates, and special security measures.

DSCC notifies the U.S. Marshals Service of the prison assignment determination upon completion. Inmates are routed for transfer to their designated institution and then transported there by U.S. Marshals.

Inmates' custody levels and security points can change with time. After serving a few years, the inmate's age may dictate a reduced prison security level. Conversely, if the inmate gets convicted of a disciplinary infraction, this will increase their security points, perhaps enough to raise their security level, necessitating relocation to another facility. The inmate's case manager can recalculate their prison security level as needed.

The Bureau of Prisons classifies prisons by one of five security levels:

Minimum Security – Minimum-security prisons, called Federal Prison Camps, are the lowest security level within the Federal Bureau of Prisons. Minimum-security camps house white-collar inmates and prisoners incarcerated for drug offenses. These camps have dormitory housing, a low staff-to-inmate ratio, and limited or no perimeter fencing.

Low Security – Federal Correctional Institutions (FCIs) are low-security federal prisons. These facilities house the largest percentage of federal inmates. Low-security federal prisons have fences, electronic security systems, a higher staff-to-inmate ratio, and tighter control over inmate movement. These prisons feature double-fenced perimeters with electronic detection systems.

FCI inmates generally have less than twenty years remaining on their sentence. Prisoners may have a history of violence, but BOP may transfer to medium-security federal prisons those caught fighting, drinking, using drugs, or committing severe infractions.

Unlike Federal Prison Camps, BOP houses sex offenders and higher-risk inmates in at least low-security, safe facilities where there is minimal violence and gang involvement.

FCIs tend toward overcrowding. Inmates live in a dormitory- or cubicle-style setting, though some low-security federal prisons have a limited number of cells.

Though overcrowded, these facilities offer a relaxed, although loud, atmosphere. The most significant downside of FCIs is the dormitory-style housing. This results in limited privacy with communal bathrooms and shower facilities. Like the other security levels, inmates can play sports, watch TV, practice religion, and further their education.

Institutional disturbances in low-security prisons are rare, if not nonexistent. Even while gangs are present, they may not be prevalent. Inmates convicted of sexual offenses and those who have testified against others are, for the most part, safe. Inmates do not need to be gang members to remain safe.

Low-security inmates tend to be middle-of-the-road, having less violent histories and being less concerned with prison politics. While not as safe as minimum-security prisons, they have lower levels of sexual abuse and are far less violent than U.S. Penitentiaries.

Medium Security – Medium-security federal prisons house inmates in cells and have strengthened perimeters, a high staff-to-inmate ratio, and enhanced security controls over inmates. Double-fenced perimeters with electronic detection systems surround them. Prison staff exert greater control over the inmate population.

Medium-security federal prisons house all manner of federal inmates, including those convicted of federal drug offenses, white-collar crimes, sexual offenses, and others.

Inmates designated to medium-security prisons may have a history of violence. A history of escape, in-prison alcohol and substance abuse, or a lengthy disciplinary record may also cause an inmate to be assigned to a medium-security prison.

Inmates designated to a medium-level prison may have more than twenty years remaining on their sentence but must have less than thirty years left to serve. However, BOP sometimes assigns lifer-term inmates to this security level.

Most medium-security prisons nearly overflow with inmates housed in cells. Many medium-security inmates reside in two- or three-person cells, while some institutions supplement these with four-, six-, ten- or even twelve-bed cells.

Cells have steel bunk beds bolted into a wall. Additionally, cells have a metal toilet/sink/water fountain combo, a steel desk bolted into a wall, small lockers, and fluorescent lights.

Televisions, phones, and computers are in a central area of the housing unit. Staff bolt TVs into structural beams, and inmates use their AM/FM radios to tune to a particular channel to hear. Different inmate groups, such as white, black, Hispanic, and others, will often claim control over certain TVs.

Medium security-level inmates may access educational classes, health services, recreation departments, and religious services. These inmates may also visit with their families on designated days. Officers strip-search these inmates following visitation.

Due to the large inmate populations housed at the medium-security level, violence is more prevalent than in lower-security settings.

Unlike low-security institutions, at rougher medium-security federal prisons, the inmate culture informally dictates that convicts must be members of a gang to remain safe. At these institutions, inmates are not safe staying independent.

In many mediums, prisoners convicted of sex offenses (and others deemed unsavory) might have difficulty remaining in the general population. At facilities considered rougher than others, sex offenders, informants, and homosexual inmates may be 'checked in' to protective custody for their safety.

High Security – U.S. Penitentiaries (USP) are high-security prisons housing the most dangerous federal prisoners. Also known as federal penitentiaries, high-security federal prisons, and maximum-security prisons, these institutions house a small percentage of the federal prison system's population.

United States prisons have highly secured perimeters, including walls or reinforced fences. Inmates reside in one- or two-person cells. Other than the ADX Florence administrative maximum facility, high-security federal prisons have the highest staff-to-inmate ratio and the tightest control of inmates. Guard towers staffed by rifle-wielding guards surround these prisons.

Federal prisons are extremely dangerous, and violence is commonplace. These facilities house high-risk inmates with significant prison misconduct, violence, and escape histories.

United States Penitentiaries house disruptive and often violent inmates. Many federal penitentiary inmates can be said to pose a threat to prison staff, each other, and society.

More than half of all assaults on inmates take place in these high-security prisons, as do most assaults on staff. Prison gangs tend to run USPs, and as a result, fights and stabbings are commonplace.

BOP must place Federal prisoners with more than thirty years remaining on their sentence in a U.S. prison. Inmates housed in these prisons tend to be younger and have high-security point totals.

United States Penitentiaries are some of the world's most violent and inhumane prisons. Constant tension and conflict infuse these facilities. Racial hatred and turf disputes are common as well. Violence, drug use, and abuse at the hands of prison guards and prisoners are systemic. Gangs run the compounds, and only the most hardened and brazen survive in high-security prisons. It is no wonder many of these inmates have long histories of committing violent crimes inside and outside prison.

In the event of a conflict, inmates at minimum-security federal prison camps may talk tough to one another. At the low-security level, prisoners may shove each other. At the medium-security level, altercations may result in punches and more. Inmates at high-security prisons don't have fistfights; rather, they stab each other with shanks.

The culture in high security prisons is more akin to a war zone than a correctional facility. Inmates often don't engage in rational thought. They think in terms of power, fear, and coercion. Daily interactions are grounded in manipulation and an abstract and distorted concept of respect.

A common theme among high-security federal prison cultures is group affiliation. While individuals outside prison may consider gang affiliation to be a net negative, gang associations are necessary to survive in these facilities.

To high-security inmates, gang affiliation is a means of protection and respect. Without it, inmates expose themselves to abject violence. Guaranteed violence comes with it, as does a group of prisoners who will retaliate on behalf of the affiliated inmate, creating some level of additional protection.

Lockdowns at high-security prisons are common due to institutional violence. These lockdowns frequently occur, resulting in inmates being confined to their cells until prison security staff believe the threat has passed.

Administrative Security – The Federal Bureau of Prisons categorizes federal prisons with special missions as Administrative Security Institutions, sometimes called 'Ad-Sec" or 'ADX.' These facilities house inmates of all security levels. These include Metropolitan Detention Centers, Metropolitan Correctional Centers, Federal Detention Centers, and Federal Medical Centers.

Administrative security facilities have unique missions, including detaining pretrial federal criminal defendants, treating inmates with severe or chronic medical problems, and containing federal prisoners deemed dangerous, violent, or escape prone.

The prison's mission, not the inmate's security points or custody classification, defines a prison's designation as an administrative-security prison. BOP can house inmates from high-security federal prisons to minimum-security camps together at these facilities.

CHAPTER THIRTY

Seagoville Satellite Camp

"'Vengeance is mine, says the Lord.'
Unless, of course, you can sneak
your future ex-husband an
excruciatingly painful huge keister."

—— **Kim Emerson**

FOR OUR CONVICTIONS from the Colombia Operation, the court sentenced William Winchester and me to three years in the Federal Correctional Institution Seagoville, a low-security United States Federal prison for male inmates. Specifically, the judge assigned us to the minimum security satellite camp, where we would serve eighteen months of the full sentence of three years.

At the camp, I ate three square meals daily but still lost weight. There were guards and a barbed wire fence, but no razor wire on the top. The facility had a three-par pitch-and-put golf course and tennis courts. In addition, there was a psychiatrist on call to talk to as needed.

If you had to go to prison, this camp would not be the worst place you could go.

William Winchester and I worked in the kitchen while in the camp. I was the head cook and he was the lead vegetable preparer. We were both vegetarians and were responsible for purchasing the fresh produce for the camp. We would go to the farmer's market to select the vegetables with BOP personnel in a one-ton flatbed prison truck with wooden slat rails. When we returned from there, we would have secreted some contraband among the produce.

When we went to the farmer's market, someone in the camp would call my wife, Kim, to tell her when we would be there. We would shop, pack our purchases into boxes, and load them onto the truck's bed. Then, while we were walking around with the kitchen guard overseeing us, Kim would walk up to the truck, open a box, and hide a pound of pot inside. Additionally, we knew a lot of ex-convicts on the outside. We would tell them when we were going to the farmer's market, and they would come down and put two or three ounces of pot in the vegetable boxes for us.

When we finished our shopping, one of the supervisors paid for the produce, and then we returned to camp. At the prison gate, the guards stopped the truck and inspected it. They opened the hood, looked around the engine compartment, and then held a mirror under the chassis to ensure that no one had hidden anything and that no one was hiding under there.

Then, the Warden came out to watch the inspection. He picked out a random box and began searching through it. Unfortunately, that particular box just happened to contain the pot Kim had hidden. Fortunately, before the Warden found the weed, William ran up, snatched the box out of the Warden's hands, and carried it off to the refrigerator in the kitchen. Amazingly, the Warden had no response. So now, we had a pound of pot inside, which we could give to the other inmates. When charging twenty-five dollars for a tiny bit of pot that could fit inside the cap from a tube of Chapstick® we were sitting in the 'Fat Seat.'

Winchester and I were on landscaping duty for a while, working under the hot sun. We did the mowing and kept the grounds neat and clean. There was a shed behind the Warden's house with a bathroom that inmates could use. I kept a jar of Vaseline® hidden in the shed's rafters. There was also a hollowed-out cedar tree trunk on the Warden's property, where I buried an empty one-pound coffee can.

Shamus Fitzpatrick would come by sometimes and drop off a load of pot already in pieces in a McDonald's bag. I would retrieve the bag and bury it in the coffee can. Then, from time to time, we would dig up the can and get enough pot to make four or five 'keisters.'

The pot we received was already clean and baggy, but we would use a vice to compact it as much as possible. Then we would wrap it with electrician's tape in the shape of a joint, put it in another baggie, wrap it again with electrician's tape, and then make it smooth, tight, and as small as possible. Finally, we would apply the Vaseline® and stick it up our 'keisters.' Thus, the name. When at our destination, we would go inside and shit it out. You have to wonder how many people in that prison contracted Hepatitis A from these 'keisters.'

Sometimes, our friends would come for a visit. They would throw out a bag of pot on the side of the road. Then, when we were mowing in that area, we would retrieve it and bring it in. Once, two or three months before being released from the camp, William Winchester got a leave. On his way back to camp, he crawled up to the fence near where he always mowed and left three or four ounces of pot by the fence. The next time he worked in the yard, he picked it up and brought it inside.

Kim finally had her revenge against me for all the shit I had put her through. She brought me a huge keister she had made that looked like a fuckin' dildo! It was long and bulbous on one end. I almost passed out trying to carry it in my ass because it was pressing against a blood vessel or something. Finally, I said, "I gotta go! Now!"

Of course, I lived in the farthest building from the visitation area. So, I hurried off as quickly and as carefully as I could. I stopped at the first building I could get to and headed straight for the toilet. As I was nearing the building, I started to pass out and barely managed to make it to the bathroom. As soon as I slid my britches down, that sumbitch shot out of my ass like a rocket. I was sitting there sweating and almost passing out when it escaped. "Gawd Almighty! Thank you, Jesus. Thank you." If I had tripped and fallen on the compound with that thing in my ass, the guards would have caught me bringing in contraband, which would cost me another conviction.

CHAPTER THIRTY-ONE

Shelby County Jail

*"The cruelty perpetrated by one human being
on another in the Shelby County Jail defied
description. Mere words could not convey
the shock, the smell of fear, or the pain suffered."*

—— **Jay Emerson**

THE POLICE HELD ME in the Shelby County Jail in Memphis, Tennessee while I awaited my court date for the Memphis Operation arrest. It would be a gross understatement to say that Hell manifested itself on earth in the form of the Shelby County Jail. *Newsweek* magazine and TV series *20/20* both stated that the Shelby County Jail was the worst maintained and operated county jail in the United States.

The cruelty perpetrated by one human being on another in the Shelby County Jail defied description. Mere words could not convey the shock, the smell of fear, or the pain suffered. You must witness these things firsthand to truly appreciate these feelings.

When the grill opened to let me into the section I would occupy for the coming months, I noted that there was not a single white man in the crowd of forty or so inmates. My three co-defendants, Buck Cameron, Bernie Rémy, Carl Cochran, and I were the only white men in a sea of black men.

We were on the third floor of the building, where all Federal holdovers stayed until the setting of their bail. If the Magistrate did not set bail, you would sit in a five-by-eight cell to await your conviction or release. Within the confines of the cell, there was a toilet, a wash basin, and an overhead light that shined twenty-four hours a day.

Walking to my new address that day in January 1989, on the hallway floor, I noticed urine and blood running together, pooling in the depressions of the tile floor, only to be replaced with another pool of blood in another location the next day. Every day, somewhere, sometime, you would hear the screams of fear choking in the throats of those whom fate had chosen to pay their debts to the god of pain.

I did not sleep in a cell like other prisoners because of the overcrowding. Instead, I slept on the floor in the hallway for the first two weeks. I had no access to proper facilities unless, out of the generosity of a kind soul, that person would let me into his cell to use the toilet or brush my teeth.

Violence was the order of the day, as various cliques and gangs chose to inflict on others the hurt and pain they themselves had endured from society. It was a way to belittle the other man just to make themselves look bigger in their own eyes.

The tradition was for the ruling body to impose a ritual upon two selected newly admitted inmates. The ruling body inmates took the new initiates to the back of the cell area, out of sight from the guards, and forced the new initiates to fight one another. The initiates could be blood brothers, friends caught in the same sting operation, or complete strangers. They were going to fight each other tooth and nail. If they decided to stand up against the ruling party and deny them the satisfaction of the fight, the ruling party would assign four or five of their biggest and toughest members to extract the proper amount of blood from the new inmates by mercilessly beating them senseless.

Another game used to fill the monotony of the day was to identify a new black inmate, a 'brother,' who appeared to have done rather well on the street dealing the drug of his choice, as evidenced by his gold-capped teeth spelling out his name. Next, another 'brother' would lure that individual to the back of the room under the guise of camaraderie. Then, in a dark, violent corner of the unit, they would knock the unfortunate brother unconscious and hold him down while his 'brothers' pulled and knocked the gold teeth out of his head. Finally, they would mail the extracted gold teeth to their friends on the street to sell them on the gold market for the bounty they held.

Finally, after about two months of this existence, I bribed one of the medical officials into sending me to the second floor, where I was in a ward for a trumped-up heart ailment. While there, I heard the story of a young man who found a nine-millimeter cartridge. With ingenuity and the determination of an animal trapped in a snare frantically gnawing his paws off to get away, the man rigged a homemade zip gun using a toothbrush for the striker of the primer cap. Then he calmly stuck the weapon in his mouth and blew the top portion of his head all over three people as they watched with rapt attention the suicide take place.

Was this justified? In the heat of desperation, I viewed the act as a last-ditch effort to free himself from the pain of emotional and physical trauma.

The medical ward was like walking onto the set of the 1975 film, *One Flew Over the Cuckoo's Nest,* and seeing the whole crew, including Nurse Ratched, on hand. There was violence here also. There was no escaping that anywhere.

In the medical ward, I witnessed one of the most atrocious acts against a human being I have ever seen. Keep in mind that the staff of the medical ward maintained the mentally ill as well as the physically ill.

One individual would walk the cell area having full-fledged conversations with himself. All the other inmates would leave the mentally disordered inmates alone, afraid they would also contract the mentally diseased germ just by breathing in the same air as they did.

On the day of the incident, the chow hall served a form of yardbird, loosely referred to as 'chicken,' though you would swear it was road kill – maybe armadillo or skunk. So, on the day they served 'chicken,' we were anxious to eat, for this was the house specialty compared to the other meals served.

The food in the Shelby County Jail? Let me say they fed the zoo animals better than they did us. You can imagine the effect this food had on my system since before my incarceration, I was a vegetarian for thirteen years. Pitiful.

Well, on this day of 'chicken,' people would trade that once-a-week meal for favors rendered earlier in the week, and payment was due on the night they served the chicken. Chicken that we bartered and exchanged just as gold and legal tender would be on the streets of the free world.

The chicken traders marked this particular mental case to learn a lesson many investment counselors have experienced due to the mismanagement of funds. The system squashes them like ants.

Due to the lack of concentration, forgetfulness, or just plain stupidity, that week, this poor sonovabitch, had traded off his weekly ration of chicken to two different people for two different favors.

Somebody would get shorted his due portion when the 'legal tender chicken' funds were divided and distributed. Somebody would end up without his piece of capital – his share of the frickin' chicken!

The day this happened, I was in my cell, where I had moved sometime earlier, sitting on my bunk, drifting in and out of my own little world, mind traveling, wishing I was somewhere else besides where destiny had decided to seat me.

It became quiet, which rarely happens in a cell block with forty or more inmates living together. The quiet was the foretelling of doom, the calm that manifests itself before the sounds of the hooves of Hell's Riders coming over the horizon. The silence that comes from the beast stalking its prey.

You could feel the tension in the air just as you could feel the breeze blowing on your face even though you couldn't see it. You could feel the adrenalin elevating with the tension rising just as the sun in the east rises to meet each day.

You could tell that pain was about to be born with its misshapen face, staring at you with a grin of selfish desire. 'Evil' was entering the room.

The wolves circled their prey for the evening's feast, with the mental case oblivious to the attention being given to him by the circling band hungry for action. After delivering the chicken to his first customer, this man would pay his second customer either with chicken, which he could not, or with blood, his own.

Finally, the wolves cornered the moron in front of my cell, and I was brought back from the dreams of escape to the reality of the here and now. With a faking gesture to draw the attention of the mental dwarf in one direction, another inmate stepped up from behind to strike him from the blind spot, and with the strike came the sound of knuckles meeting soft flesh behind the ear. The idiot knew he was locked in the jaws of hurt and pain, and shock and bewilderment followed him down to the floor while the wolves attacked, ravenous for their share of meat and blood.

They kicked, stomped, and beat with their fists this poor soul who walked through life as a disabled slave to society's wishes, with not enough mental capacity to even understand that death was stalking him.

The other inmates craned their necks to see who the center of attention was, then turned a blind eye, a deaf ear, or a cold back to the destruction of a human being. Even I could not jump into this pool of anger, wielding the sword of truth and love to save this unfortunate soul. There is a saying that God protects drunks and fools. Where in the hell was God this time? And why was He not protecting this poor fool?

As the pack slowly exhausted their energy on this man, I sat on my bunk, looking dumbfounded by the brutality and hate being leveled at this individual. The man was lying in pain, not five feet from the entrance to my cell. Then, with a movement of desperation, he rolled over on his side and faced me, and for a second that seemed to freeze motion and time into eternity, our eyes met and locked onto each other. We each threw the windows of our souls open as we looked deeply into each other's being. While looking into this man's eyes, imprisoned with the contact of his soul, I saw a wolf coming for the killing blow. I could say nothing and do nothing, frozen as this demon in human form drew back his foot and, with the power of a football player kicking the ball off the tee, let loose with the fury of misguided hate and kicked the man in the head directly under his chin. The sound of the contact between the foot and the chin was not what the five senses of my body expected to pick up to store in my memory cells. No, the explosive shock wave, the kinetic energy, and the sound will always ring in my soul and memory.

The idiot's head snapped back at an angle that was so unnatural. Indeed, I imagined from the sound that the blow must have broken his neck and destroyed his life. Then, with the man lying on the floor, blood seeping from the mouth, ear, and nose and pooling around his body, the frenzy and the suffering were over. The inhumane act of hate had fulfilled its hunger and left with its belly full of this man's pain, hurt, and destruction.

As this sound and shock wave of the blow echoed over and over inside my head, I sat there looking into this poor man's eyes. He was not yet dead, but still breathing, as evidenced by the blood bubbles coming with each small exhale. Yet, he would never realize why he had paid such a terrible price this night.

The guards immediately locked down the cell and transported the poor soul to the hospital.

The staff at Shelby were horrified and angrily showed their frustration as to 'why?' He was a mental retard. Why would you do this?

No one cared. This poor man's life had ended, all for a chicken. He would not be remembered, and there would be no consequences for his attackers.

Just another day in the Shelby County Jail.

Only once in my original incarceration did I try to describe the horror I felt in the Shelby County Jail. When I did write about the event, the pain was so intense I could not stop my hands from shaking while writing the story. While going through the experiences of Shelby County, I forced them to the back of my mind, shutting them away behind a locked door buried deep within the confines of my subconscious mind. On that day in December 1990, I pulled the locks from the door that held these experiences buried and, upon releasing them, penned my thoughts and moments on paper. I realized that what I had liberated from behind the door of my subconscious mind would always be, and there was no way for me to purge the experiences from my soul. I was hurt so emotionally from the experiences and through the act of putting them on paper that tears welled up in my eyes when I finished writing.

One year after I departed from its walls, the Federal government deregulated the Shelby County Jail and ordered it to close its doors to Federal prisoners due to these barbaric conditions.

CHAPTER THIRTY-TWO

Promises Not Kept

*"It is better not to promise anything
than to promise something and not do it."*

—— **Ecclesiastes 5:5 (NIV)**

THE SHELBY COUNTY JAIL WAS DEREGULATED, while I was still awaiting my trial, so I moved to the Clarendon County Jail, and Buck moved to the Monroe County Jail, both in Clarendon, Arkansas. Later, he moved to FCI Memphis, a medium-security prison in Memphis, Tennessee.

After our arrests, Sheriff's officers took us to the precinct office in downtown Memphis for interrogation. This would be the first felony conviction for Carl Cochran and Bernie Rémy, so they faced a minimum sentence of ten years. However, it would be the third felony conviction for Buck Cameron and myself, so that would classify us as 'career criminals' facing thirty years and maybe even life.

Carl, Bernie, and I were inclined to plead guilty, but Buck wanted to go to trial and fight the charges. Eventually, Buck persuaded them to go along, but I held out. He persisted in trying to convince me to go along with him by promising, "When I'm out, I'll come for you because I got all this money in my stock. I'll sell our company, the furniture store and funeral home. I'll sell my stock, and I'll rescue you. That's a promise."

Yeah, right.

I pleaded guilty, and the jury found Buck, Carl, and Bernie guilty on both counts. The two girls riding with Buck testified against him and he ended up with an enhanced sentence to include life imprisonment without parole.

In August and September 1990, Buck wrote at least five letters to me while he was in FCI Memphis, and I was still in Clarendon County Jail for our Memphis Operation.

Skipping over the usual mundane greetings and endings, excerpts from the text of these letters expose some insights into Buck's concerns, mindset, and general character, or lack thereof, during his first time in prison.

August 23, 1990

Things aren't so bad here at FCI Memphis, but they aren't as good as Monroe County Jail. We stay locked down most of the time and very seldom get to go outside. We do get to use the phone, though. Big deal, huh?

For some reason, these people had me listed as an escape risk because someone wrote the U.S. Marshals and told them I was planning to have my family break me out of jail. I can't imagine who. Probably one of those Mexicans. What a stupid and dirty thing to do. But now, it's on my record, and I am considered an escape risk. Great, huh? That's all I need as if I didn't have enough problems as it is.

When I was leaving Monroe, the Sheriff was there and was totally surprised that the Marshals were also there. In other words, whoever told that lie about me went straight to the Marshals and not through the Sheriff. Then, when I got here, one of the officers said, "So you're the one who was planning on escaping with the help of your family."

What a bunch of bullshit.

It seems like everything and everyone has turned against me. It's a dog-eat-dog world. That's for sure. I'm having my ups and downs. Sometimes I feel like just hanging it up, but then I remind myself that as long as I'm still sucking air, I have a chance.

August 28, 1990

Even though you and I seem to have our disagreements, I miss the company of you and Carl. You will always be like a brother to me, no matter what.

I hear that you all are going to move over here soon. Micheal arrived today, and there are still ten extra beds. There is a lot of lockdown time, but all the milk you can drink and the food is somewhat better.

I talked to Mike about buying my stock, and he is trying to buy it way too cheap, but I promised you, him, and your mother that I would sell at any price. So, he offered me twenty-five to thirty thousand for my stock, which is about half its worth.

I spoke to Attorney J. Stephen Cooper and explained the situation to him. He still believes that we won't even need the ten thousand, but if we do, I will sell to save my ass as well as yours. You can bet your ass and mine on that. I have more to lose timewise than anyone. I just want to wait until the last, until we really need it, to sell.

This is an excellent opportunity for Mike to end up with the Tanner business. So, if he is going to buy, he will buy then as well as now. Also, the apartment looks like it will sell, and I will get around five thousand for my part. Things are looking up.

But anyway, to answer your question, I will sell if we need to, when we need to. My ass is at stake too. I would also like to tell Assistant U.S. Attorney Timothy R. DiScenza to fuck off. But I understand your position.

September 2, 1990

A guy came back from court today and had overheard DiScenza bragging about how he was gonna give me a life sentence. Great, huh?

Could you get me a number for Carl's lawyer, Attorney John R. Smith? I have some questions I would like to ask him. I'm still unsure whose side Cooper is on anymore. One day, he seems to be on my side; the next, I really don't know. I would appreciate some advice from Smith.

Don't worry about me selling stock. I will as soon as need be.

September 7, 1990

Thinking about how I miss Monroe County Jail. Never thought I would think such a thought, but I do. I miss you guys for the companionship, but I also miss Monroe County. I miss the outside time more than anything else. We get to go out, but only for one hour and it's really noisy. No peace at all. At least they lock us down at night. Thank God for that. But all-in-all, Monroe County was better, I think.

There is only one other white guy here, who happens to be my roommate, and he may be leaving in a couple of weeks. He is in for money laundering a million and a half dollars. He has big-time legal connections and is trying to get me an appeal bond, which I think is impossible, but what the hell? At this point, I'll try anything.

When I got my pre-sentence report with the big 'life, no parole,' I went into shock. I knew it was coming but seeing it in black and white really set me back.

How and why are we in this position? I guess only God knows. The reason is a stupid mistake, but karma is also involved. I can't figure it out.

I plan on having Cooper call the Marshals to see if they can move me to the John M. Wynne Unit, a state prison in Huntsville [Texas]. I don't think they will, but they might. It's just that after my roommate leaves, and if you all don't come, I'll be going nuts for conversation. But I'll make it, one way or another.

Maybe they sent me over here because of something I said over the phone or wrote in a letter, which was all bullshit. But it just goes to show you have to be careful with what you say or write. Someone could take something wrong, and 'BOOM!' you get moved.

September 11, 1990

Right after I got my pre-sentence report back with life on it, I asked Cooper if we could cooperate with only the information about the Lamberto and Quintero thing and the customs agent deal. He immediately shut that down and said that they would not go for it. It has to be an all-or-nothing type of deal. So, we are back to square one. It was just a momentary freakout on my part. It probably would have been my death warrant anyway.

Yeah, so much for promises made and promises [not] kept. *From the time of the initial offer, I suspected that Buck never intended to get me out with the proceeds from the sale of his interest in the business, unless it would suit his needs. It was just a bargaining chip he waved in my face to hold me off.*

CHAPTER THIRTY-THREE

Messing About in Boats

"Believe me, my young friend;
there is nothing – absolutely nothing –
half so much worth doing
as simply messing about in boats."

—— **Kenneth Grahame**
The Wind in the Willows [6]

AFTER MY SENTENCING HEARING, I moved to the United States Penitentiary Atlanta in 1990 for the first month to get my Diagnostics and then move to a more permanent facility. USP Atlanta had formerly been a high-security facility but, at that time, was low-security. Nevertheless, it still had walls that were forty feet tall and twelve feet thick. So, it was old school and an *extremely dangerous* place.

You talk about being afraid. I walked in there, and I was *scared shitless!*

Those were mean men in there, real convicts. There were inmates, and then there were convicts. Inmates were 'wussified.' Convicts were 'The Man.' They were the old school, and that's what we were.

Then all the gangbangers started flooding in. It was like, "Who can rat first?" They were inmates. Inmates were newer. I was a convict, I believed in the 'old codes' of 'honor among thieves.'

From Atlanta, I moved to FCI Texarkana, a high-security prison at the time. While I was at FCI Texarkana and had already done about six years, I spent most of my spare time on the weight pile and playing handball. I had done all there was to do in my limited environment.

Then, one day, sitting alone in my cell, I thought I would surely go insane with boredom. Trying to stay occupied, I wandered into the cell across from mine. "Hey, brother, got anything to read?"

The man reached over to a pile of magazines on a shelf, pulled one off the top, and handed it to me.

"Hmm, *WoodenBoat* magazine? I'm not familiar with that one."

"Good stuff," he said. "I have a subscription."

I thumbed through the pages of the magazine. On the cover was a photo of a magnificent all-mahogany classic Gentleman's Racer literally leaping out of the water. Time stopped for me. I developed a myopic focus on that cover photo.

As I discovered through my reading, a Gentleman's Racer is a rare classic all-mahogany wooden boat with a high-powered engine. The cockpit was located in the very aft end of the boat. These incredible vessels are characterized by long, narrow, sleek bows, which cover almost the entire length of the boat, except for the cockpit area. From bow to stern, the magnificently grained mahogany hulls of these boats are faired and sanded, and then stained, sealed, varnished, and polished to a brilliant sheen. They were developed as thoroughbreds built for boat racing. And they are literal and magnificent works of art.

Oh, my God! Destiny shot an arrow into my heart. Then it leaned over and whispered, "This is the plan for your life."

I thanked my neighbor and returned to my cell with the magazine, where I immersed myself in it, reading it multiple times from cover to cover and digesting it whole. I had never been a big reader beyond mind-numbing pulp fiction from Louis L'Amour and Stephen King. But I was absolutely intrigued by what I saw.

As I sat in my cell gazing at the beautiful ships, sailboats, and other sea craft in the magazine, I visualized a vast expanse of ocean and dreamed of one day sailing around the world on my own boat. For me, the ocean represented the ultimate freedom. On the water, a sea captain is his own democracy, the president of his own country, the supreme being with no one to answer to but God.

Oh, if I ever have the chance... I thought as I imagined the feel of the wind on my skin and the smell of the salt air.

Thus began my love for wooden boats, all encapsulated by a beautiful dream.

Contained among the pages of the magazine were plans for building an eleven-foot shellback dinghy. The article gave step-by-step instructions, diagrams, and illustrations. I knew I couldn't build an actual dinghy in prison, but perhaps I could create a model.

The idea of building this boat ignited my imagination and creativity, which I was not previously aware that I had. But I was in there. That's for sure.

I began the process of constructing a model boat despite having next to nothing in the way of tools or materials to work with. My tool kit consisted of a disposable razor, a broken needle for a miniature drill, and a pair of toenail clippers, which became my most precious instrument. I used the cardboard backing from writing tablets to shape the boat's hull. Scraps of wood and sandpaper found in trash cans or small containers of glue that I could trade a pack of cigarettes for became valuable commodities. I pounded and flanged clipped wires, twisted sewing thread for riggings, and made doorknobs from nail heads. The tips of ballpoint pins became pintles and gudgeons. A torn-up T-shirt served as a sail. All these items I found from workshops and industries.

After about eighty hours of labor, I had it – a perfect shellback dinghy that could fit right in the palm of my hand.

I painted the boat and named it *Diane* after my mother, who had remained devoted to me despite my incarceration. I presented it to her as a gift on her next visit.

I had discovered a way to occupy my time and maintain my sanity for the remainder of my days in prison. I continued to build model ships, even christening one of my fifteen boats, *Sanitee*.

I began building model antique wooden sailing ships from these and other plans I found in various *WoodenBoat* issues. Fascinated by this new hobby and having a seemingly infinite amount of time on my hands and no other responsibilities or pursuits to occupy myself, I threw myself into the task despite the minimal tools and materials I had available to construct the boats.

In prison, you're dead. It's all about maintaining your sanity. You must have dreams, whether they ever truly manifest themselves or not. My only means of escape were my hopes and dreams of one day building my own boat and sailing it around the world.

Needless to say, I had plenty of time to perfect my craft of building model ships, and I admit that after six long years of building model ships, I was beyond ready for the interaction and hands-on experience of the real thing.

After that, everything I did was for the furtherance of my boatbuilding.

The next day, I quit my job as a clerk and went to the wood shop.

"I don't care what I have to do," I said. "I'll sweep the floor if that's what you need. I want to transfer here because I need somebody to teach me how to use power tools." I had never used a power tool because I grew up as one of those country club kids.

"I want you to teach me how to use these tools because someday, I want to build a boat."

After spending months in the wood shop working with saws and planers and such, I discovered a side benefit of working there, which was that we made our hooch in the wood shop. And hooch was important in prison. We had an old, non-functioning planer/jointer mounted on an enclosed metal box. The Occupational Safety and Health Administration (OSHA) required everything in the shop to have a vacuum exhaust. The prison bolted all the major tools and equipment to the floor, but we could lift the planer/jointer off the bolts. Then we could put our hooch in there and set the planer/jointer back down, and the vacuum system would take all the smell right to the outside. Ventilation of the hooch was vital because it smelled like baby shit. If an inmate so much as opened a bag of hooch to check on its progress, he risked detection.

There were four or five of us in the shop. We would put our hooch under the planer/jointer every week and pick it up on Friday. We had to leave a little bit of product behind each time because it contained the yeast. We just added more grapefruit, which we could buy at the commissary, put in more sugar, and let it ferment until the following week. We would come to get it the next Friday and slam the whole thing. Then, we would wobble to our cells for the four o'clock count. On the way, we would be like, "Woo-hoo," right in front of everybody. "Woo-hoo."

Hooch typically has an alcohol by volume of five percent, which is stronger than most lagers.

<<<>>>

Then, in 1995, the Federal Bureau of Prisons reclassified FCI Texarkana as a low-security facility. Unfortunately, I wasn't yet qualified to be in a low-security facility, so they sent me to Federal Correctional Institution Three Rivers, a medium-security facility eighty-five miles south of San Antonio. The prison itself was bigger than the local town of the same name.

Fortunately, they allowed me to take my boatbuilding stuff along.

When I got to the Three Rivers Art Department, they said, "What do you think you're going to do with all that stuff?"

And so, I explained to them what I was doing, and they said, "Well, we'll see how it goes."

Thankfully, they let me continue my boatbuilding activities there at Three Rivers.

I had a friend there, Mark, whose father had been a general contractor building big residential neighborhoods in El Paso. Then, Mark and his dad, Howard, got into smuggling and made a lot of money before getting busted and caught holding ten million dollars in a closet. Now, they both were doing time.

The supervisor of the Art Department knew my friend Mark and had pity on him because his father, Howard, was serving his time at another institution. The supervisor needed an experienced wood worker, so he contacted the Bureau of Prisons to have Howard transferred to Three Rivers.

And then he stuck me with that cranky old sonovabitch from El Paso, Howard. However, he came in and fixed up the whole shop to make it a functional wood shop. I needed him to teach me how to keep my fingers. And he did a good job at that, and we built cabinets and tables.

Howard also helped me build my first model sailing ship, a two-masted Gloucester schooner from the 1890s to the 1910s era. He allowed me to do that in his shop so long as nobody else saw it. "Inmates can see it, but as long as none of the supervisors see it, we should be okay."

"As long as you get your job done," he said, "then if you have free time, I don't care what you do. It's good to keep yourself occupied. Idle hands are the devil's workshop."

I'm not sure, but I think someone else may have already coined that phrase.

There were a lot of Hispanics in Three Rivers because it was an Immigration and Naturalization Service (INS) facility.

Mark's father, Howard, was diligent about sharpening his wood chisels, and he spent a lot of time doing it. Then he came in one day and found one of the Mexicans knocking a hole in a cinder block wall with one of his newly sharpened chisels. Well, he just went berserk. "GODDAMMIT!" he screamed, "I'M NOT FUCKIN' DOING THIS SHIT ANYMORE! YOU BUNCH OF UNGRATEFUL BASTARDS!"

He snatched the chisel from the Mexican and waved it at him threateningly. The Mexican obviously had no appreciation for the care that Mark's father had taken of his tools.

I knew I would build a boat someday, but I first wanted to know what problems I might encounter. Then, I thought that if I built one on a smaller scale and experienced the problems first-hand, maybe when I got to the full scale, they wouldn't be so challenging to handle. And so, I really got into making scale model ships. First, I subscribed to *WoodenBoat* magazine and had it sent to me directly. Eventually, I accumulated stacks of issues. Each issue contained a design section with the schematics and drawings I needed to make my models and half-hull models.

Soon, word got around about my model boatbuilding, and others became interested. So, I brought other inmates into my informal program. I taught them joinery work and construction skills. This training gave these inmates a great sense of accomplishment and pride and kept them busy. Many gang members in the program would eventually do more with building their boats than they would with their gang.

"Hey, Concha! We're gonna go fuck with the white boys. You down for that?"

"What for?" Concha asked.

"Whaddaya mean, what for? They're white motherfuckers. Isn't that enough?"

"Well, maybe. But count me out this time. I got something else to do."

"You got something else do to, Concha?"

"Yeah, man. I'm building my boat. Leave me alone."

The gang member looked at him side-eyed, but then left him to his own. He was a bit confused and bewildered. Yet, also curious about what Concha was talking about.

A Christian fellow in San Francisco was building a boat of his own. He planned to load it up with blue jeans, shoes, and Bibles and sail it down to Mexico on a mission trip. He had heard of my program and wanted to promote it in any way he could by supplying us with money and tools.

Unfortunately, bureaucratic red tape enveloped that idea. This fellow had to send his donations to the Federal government in Washington, D.C., and let them allocate them however they wanted. Consequently, my group didn't get much of his contributions. However, we got noticed by Washington, D.C., and they came to Three Rivers to look at the program. I hoped to implement the program in other institutions, too.

After a time, the Federal government allowed me to implement a program to teach inmates in the institution how to build these model ships. So, we were building wooden model boats – intricately detailed and fully-rigged scale models. We constructed probably a couple hundred models. I completed more than sixty of these magnificent boats myself.

The prison officials were so impressed with our work on these boats that they allowed me to order tools and materials and even teach model shipbuilding classes to other inmates. Amazingly, my students included some of the most dangerous, violent, and heavily tattooed Hispanic gangbangers, who became so absorbed in their creations as to become oblivious to the realities of the world surrounding them in their incarceration.

I published an article about what we were doing with our program in the January/February 1998 issue of *WoodenBoat* magazine. The main photo for that article was of a fellow named Mike Rangel, one of those gang members with tattoos all over his body, standing with the model he had built, just as proud as he could be.

Eventually, the program grew to about ten to fifteen people. It was a great little program. It was an escape. We could sit there for hours and hours, focusing intently on building our model ships. Eventually, it would get to the point where someone would tap us on the shoulder and say, "It's time to leave."

"Oh, man, I just got here. I just got here."

But we would go to the four o'clock count, then return to the shop and get back to work.

We had our lockers, our boats, and our wood. However, when contracting with vendors to send us materials, we had to work with them through the Federal government to order and purchase. Eventually, we were getting tools sent to us: little saw tables, micro-saw tables, and drill bits, which would typically be unheard of for an inmate to have.

The administration even allowed us razor blades, knives, and chisels. The program had a budget to buy tools for a season, and every year we got more and more vendors for our wood, parts, and pieces.

CHAPTER THIRTY-FOUR

Five to One, Baby!

*"You always post a 'jigger' outside
when you're doing something sneaky like this."*

—— **Jay Emerson**

I WAS SITTING AT A TABLE eating lunch one day, and there were guys here, here, and here [pointing to positions at the table], maybe six or eight feet away from me. All of a sudden, these guys jumped off, and then you got a commotion over here. When that started, everybody at the table stood up and backed away. But I just sat there and kept on eating. I was hungry.

I looked over, and one guy had a knife sticking in the back of his neck and coming out the front of his throat, and his attacker was trying to pull it out so he could stab him again. The stabbed guy grabbed his attacker's hands and then stood up and pushed, and he was on top of the guy who had jabbed the knife in him. That guy was still trying to pull the knife out so he could stab him again.

I'm telling you, man, everybody scrambled. But I didn't get up. I just kept on eating. I was hungry.

People backed away. The guards came in and slammed people, trying to get control of the situation.

They sat the victim down, and blood was gushing out of his throat, soaking his shirt, and pouring all over the floor. But you know what? That knife missed his windpipe *and* his jugular vein! It was a miracle, I tell you.

So, the victim was sitting there at the table, shaking, and going into shock. That knife was just sticking out of his throat right there, and they were all trying to get it out.

I would think you shouldn't just pull the knife out like that so it wouldn't cause him to hemorrhage. But what do I know?

Anyway, I was eating the whole time this was going on. I was eating. I was not going to miss this, or any other meal. "Y'all can jump up if you want to, but I'm eatin'. I'm hungry."

So, I kept eating. Why not? Stabbings were normal around there. "So, what are y'all worried about?"

Later, five people were killed in that prison in one day during a riot. I was at the other end of the facility when it happened, not anywhere close to it. Thank God!

My cellie at Three Rivers was as big as a door and clean-cut like the Jersey guys. His name was Sammy, and he was from the East, a Mafia guy, although a lower-level guy. There was another Mafia guy doing time there then, one of the 'Dons' from Kansas City. He was a white-haired older fellow, but he commanded a lot of respect. And Sammy was trying to ingratiate himself with this Don.

Then Sammy came to my room one day, and he was stomping around aggressively and angrily, waving his arms, steam coming out of his ears, just mad as hell.

"I'm gonna get that sumbitch."

"What? What are you talking about?" I said.

"Yeah, that motherfucker called me a rat. He called me a snitch."

"Ah, blow it off, man. It's nothing."

For some reason, another inmate in the institution had tagged him with that accusation. Was it true? Who knew?

But the next day, Sammy tracked down his accuser on the compound and followed him out of sight, until an opportunity opened up and then fate took over. He found the guy he was hunting at the commissary, which is right next to the weight pile. Sammy picked up a 'pull-down bar,' used for triceps workouts.

Then, he walked up behind his accuser, and hit him with that bar on the back of his head. Right behind the commissary were three steps. Sammy walloped this guy so hard he fell flat back onto those steps. Then Sammy started at the guy's left foot and did not stop beating him with that bar until he had gone all the way to his head and back down the other side of his body.

His accuser was a bloody pulp and quite dead. Sammy beat that man to death with a bar from the weight pile. He killed him. It was horrible to watch. The poor guy didn't know what hit him, or who, or why.

I was at Three Rivers for a while. Then, my security requirement ran down to a point where I could move to Federal Correctional Institution Seagoville, a lower security prison.

Seagoville was good to me, and I was doing well there. I had the last room in the hallway, the best room in the facility. A big vent went up through the floor to the outside of that room. So, I could sit there, smoke pot, and blow it out the vent, and no one would be the wiser.

Pot was more readily available inside the prison. I could get it quicker and more easily than on the street. So, I smoked in there to help pass the time. But we had random, unannounced searches of our cells, and I did not want to get caught or lose my stash.

Oh, I remembered those days of yore, when I had access to 'free' pot. But now, I was stuck smoking pot that smelled like ass, having come from somebody's keister, and it still cost me twenty-five dollars for a Chapstick® cap sized bit of marijuana.

I had a great job working as a clerk for the groundskeeper, so I didn't have to work the grounds. Instead, I took care of the paperwork, which allowed me to stay up late at night.

Often, I stayed up late paper-trading in the stock market. I read *Investor's Business Daily* religiously, from cover to cover. I had six months of that paper stacked in my locker in chronological order. I focused on biotech and telecom stocks. I would choose paper trades based on three to six months of history for a particular stock. Then, I would call my mother on the pay phone in the morning to discuss the trades I wanted to make. She would place the orders for me, and I would start researching the next trade that night.

The guards allowed me to do that because many of them had asked me what they should do with their stocks. I could be that good because I had all the time in the world to work at it, so I focused my mental awareness on that. I did not have family issues or outside activities to distract me.

FCI Seagoville had been an old military base during World War II, with barracks used for holding German, Japanese, and Italian prisoners of war. These old units had a shared toilet, shower, and laundry room. We could not be locked down since no such facilities existed in our individual cells. Moreover, the guards shut the cell doors at night but did not lock them. Consequently, we could roam outside our units, although we were not supposed to be out of our cells at night.

In 2000, I was up late researching the next fifty-two week breakout stock and needed to pee. I thought I might as well also pick up the laundry I had started earlier that evening. In the laundry area,

I walked in on five Mexican gangbangers from the Border Brothers gang. They had pulled a dryer away from the wall and removed the back. I could see they were hiding their bag of hooch inside the dryer where it could get hot and ferment. I knew they would close the dryer, push it back against the wall, and let their hooch ferment for a week. And I was okay with that.

However, here is a jailhouse rule of life for the uninitiated. You always post a 'jigger' outside when doing something sneaky like this. A jigger is a lookout whose job is to tell you, "Hey! Somebody's coming. Put that shit away."

But instead, they were all in there trying to figure out who would get what and who would not.

When I walked in, they all looked up at me. *Oh, shit! What an idiot I am.* I pretended to ignore them and continued on toward my dryer, so far unmolested. I pulled my laundry out of the dryer, folded it, and loaded it into my basket, ignoring them the whole time. Then I left and returned to my cell as if nothing had happened. I guess I forgot to pee.

The next night, the guard came by on his rounds. When he walked into the laundry area, he quickly sniffed out their hooch.

Seagoville prison had been there since before World War II, and by now, those guards had seen every possible hiding spot. You had to be really creative to beat them at this game. Unfortunately, hiding your hooch inside a dryer was not very creative. So, the guard found their stash and busted them. Of course, since I had seen them hiding their hooch, the Mexicans assumed I had ratted them out.

Two nights later, I was up late again. It was about two in the morning, and all the lights were out, but I had a small table lamp lighting my papers so I could see what I was reading. Suddenly, I saw a fist coming through the light. I dodged it, jumped up, and it was on! The five Mexican gangbangers had come to my cell with the obvious intention of giving me a major ass whuppin'.

Three of them came at me first. Fortunately, I held a Second Degree Black Belt in Taekwondo from my martial arts fighting days, so I put down all three with a series of quick punches and head kicks.

I had already busted three of them, yet they managed to scramble out of my cell to rejoin their compadres, so there were still five out there. Another rule of life in the prison world is if you walk with confidence, nobody will mess with you. So, I held out my right hand, palm up, and beckoned them with my fingers to come forward. "Come on, come on. No one here gets out alive."

And so, they did, all five of them, at the same time.

I had a good friend named Hector Delphi, or the 'Greek,' as we called him. He was a big old six-foot, two hundred-fifty-pound, barrel-chested, gray-haired man who lived in the ten-man dormitory across the hall from my room.

Hector Delphi

I was lying in bed when I heard the ruckus. My buddy said, "Hey, Greek, I think they went in on Jay."

So, I came up out of the bed in my underwear. It wasn't ten yards to Jay's room, so I just barreled in. When I looked around the room, I saw five Mexican boys, and they had Jay cornered up against the wall. Jay was fighting off one of them with a chair, so I pile-drived my way in there and started grabbing Mexicans, hitting a couple of them, and throwing them out the door.

It was one of those things where if one person wants to jump on somebody in prison, whether I know them or not, I say, "Go for it," but not when it's five to one. I won't stand around and let five people whip the shit out of one guy. That's just not right. People get killed that way.

At that time, I didn't know what the scuffle was about. But the next day, I ran into the president of the Border Brothers gang. He was a little bald-headed guy, and he and I played handball together sometimes.

"Hey man," I said, "Let's go to the bleachers and talk."

And so, we went up there, and I said, "Look, man, your *vatos* went in on my buddy Jay."

He said, "Yeah, man, he snitched us out."

"He didn't snitch you out," I said, "Man, that guy's doing twenty-five years. He's done twelve of them flat already. Do you really think he's going to snitch you out? He just went in there to get his fuckin' laundry, man."

I let that sit for a minute while we watched the handball courts.

"Now, think about the boss on duty that night," I said, "He can sniff out home brew or chop with the best of them."

The Prez nodded his head in agreement.

"And that's exactly what he did do," I said, "When your *vatos* make their hooch, they permeate the fruit and everything, and then they put it behind the dryer, where it will get real hot and ferment.

"And Jay had just done his laundry and went to pick it up when the *vatos* were checking their chalk. Jay paid no attention to them. He's been around so many different units, and he's seen that shit day in and day out. But he ignored them, got his laundry, folded it, and went to his room. And the laundry was only about five doors down from Jay's room.

"Yeah. So, the boss made his rounds the next day and went in there and sniffed out the chalk.

"So, when their chalk got snatched up, they immediately blamed Jay because he had been there when they were there, and then the chalk went missing. So, they automatically accused Jay of ratting them out.

"Man, they got it all wrong," I said, "But here's the thing, brother."

This guy liked me because I had a job where I could help him. Jay had quit his job as a compound clerk in the unit, and he offered it to me. So, I took the yard job. We were responsible for making the interior grounds look perfect for visiting dignitaries from Washington, D.C. It was a cush paper job, and I got to do pretty much as I wanted, including picking up cigarette butts and trash.

And I had friends – Bloods, Crips, Border Brothers, and Mexican Mafia. They all liked me because I could give them jobs in the yard where they could get off early to go to the weight pile or play handball. So, it was one of those things I used to my advantage.

"Look, man," I said, "I'm not going to come at you with all this shit. You and I got a good working relationship because I got a lot of your *vatos* jobs."

I think he respected what I said. So, they backed off after that first night.

Jay Emerson

So, after Hector had pulled all the gangbangers off me, the attackers got up and ran down the hall, yelling back at us as they ran. Again, I beckoned them back with my hand, "Come on. Come on."

By this time, everybody on the block was out of their cells, including the President of the Border Brothers, who watched five of his soldiers running down the hall away from my cell with their tails tucked between their legs. It had to be a little embarrassing, if not infuriating, for the head boss man.

The next morning, I got up to go to breakfast.

I worked as the outside groundskeeper's clerk, which was a pretty good job. My supervisor came to me and said, "Come on, Jay, we gotta go over to the hospital. We gotta do something over there."

"Okay, let's go," I said, "Come on."

At the hospital, a guard said, "Alright, Emerson, get over there and strip down to your underwear."

"What? What?"

"Well, we heard there was a fight last night, and we need to see what you got."

Most people who get in a fight have scratches and bruises and cuts and busted knuckles.

"Oh, you have to be kidding me," I said, "Man, there was no fight last night."

I said, "There was some yellin'. Some people started yellin'. Nothing unusual, but there wasn't no fight."

But I stripped anyway. "You see anything on me? My hands ain't even hurt."

Having a second degree black belt in Taekwondo, you 'take care of things' rather quickly so as to not get hurt. I was lucky to have no busted knuckles or scratches.

"That's true. We can't see no physical evidence of a fight, but we're gonna do more investigating, so we're gonna put you in protective custody for a while in the meantime."

Oh, shit, not again. This would be the second time I had been in protective custody, commonly referred to as the 'Hole.' The first time was because I got a tattoo, as if no one else in prison had one. They called it 'disfiguring government property.' But, of course, we were government property and needed to be pretty and not disfigured. But this time, it was for my own protection, allegedly.

The Hole is a horrendous place. It's dark and hot and loud and lonely. It is worse than any human can imagine. It's literally 'hell on earth.' Unless you have been there, you can't imagine, but you never, ever want to be there if you can at all avoid it.

CHAPTER THIRTY-FIVE

Where the Journey Begins

Eventually, in the darkness,
at the bottom of the depths of my despair,
I cried out to something, someone, anyone who would listen.
In a small whimper, I said, "Help me. Please, help me."

—— Jay Emerson

AFTER I HAD SERVED more than eleven years of my sentence, a heat wave persisted in the late summer of 2000 from August to early September along the southern tier of the United States. As a result, daily high temperatures in Dallas exceeded ninety degrees every day for the entire month of August, including seven days over one hundred degrees.

In those days, only thirty percent of Texas prisons were fully air-conditioned, which did not include FCI Seagoville. As a result, temperatures inside the facility regularly reached one hundred ten degrees. The Texas Department of Criminal Justice reported that the average temperature of a unit housing area in a prison without air conditioning was usually more than eighty-nine degrees. A person can feel the impact of heat exhaustion at as low as eighty degrees. The added risk of potentially fatal heat stroke begins at ninety-one degrees. The buildings at Seagoville were originally made of red brick, which when hit by the summer sun would absorb and then radiate the heat right back. I remember walking by a building in the courtyard and twenty-five feet away, ran into a wall of heat coming from the building.

The guards had sent me to the Hole for fighting with the five Mexican gangbangers who had attacked me in my cell. The Mexicans had convinced themselves that I ratted them out after I walked in on them while they were hiding their hooch, which was not true.

Nevertheless, I was in this place again and would lose everything. Before going to the Hole, I had the best room in the whole facility, my model boatbuilding program, and a clerk's job, and I didn't have to get up early. Now, I would lose all that because those Mexican idiots wrongly thought I ratted out their hooch and the guards believed them.

The government had overcrowded the Hole to an absurd degree. Because of these conditions, the warden assigned me to a cell that was… well, simply saying it was 'horrible' would be a gross understatement. However, it was the only unit available, and it previously had been used as a temporary storage area for mops and buckets.

Late on a summer afternoon that year, the heat radiating off the brick walls of a building would feel smothering inside the institution. Because of the sweltering heat, the inmates couldn't sleep, leaving them irritable and angry at their circumstances. Tempers perpetually simmered near the boiling point. It was a miracle there were not more riots. The whole environment was insufferable.

The heat was a killer, and it tested a man to his limits. My special place in hell was below ground in a back corner of the building, where the phrase 'air circulation' held no meaning. There was only one tiny window, less than a foot square near the ceiling at ground level. Sweat soaked my clothes, the stench in the air turned my stomach, and cockroaches crawled over the floor and my body as I lay in my bunk.

The nights were the worst as I struggled desperately to sleep. Unfortunately, I never made it to sleep before two o'clock in the morning and then had to get up at four-thirty to start work in the kitchen.

To combat the unbearable heat, sometimes, I would take a cold shower wearing my bed sheets so they would get sopping wet. Then, I would lie on my bed and sleep in cold, wet sheets while the evaporation provided relief from the heat so I could go to sleep, although exhausted.

On occasion, I would flush the toilet and plug it with my bedsheet to make it overflow. Then I would lie down in the toilet water that flooded the concrete floor. The water ran everywhere, pissing off the guards and the other inmates.

I was held captive in the Hole in that oppressive heat amid the perpetual noise. Oh, my God, the noise! People yelled and screamed at the top of their lungs incessantly. We were sleep- and light-deprived, miserable, lonely, and angry. It was not the happiest place in the world.

In the wee morning hours, a week into my stay in the Hole, the suffocating heat had stolen what little air there was. I crouched on a small stainless-steel table next to the wall and craned my neck toward the lone window, desperately seeking and sucking what air I could find. Both sleep and air eluding me, I hung my head and stared blankly at the table. It was unbearable, intolerable, and inhumane.

In that moment, I whispered, "I'm so tired of this shit. I've had enough. I can't take no more."

Eventually, in the darkness, at the bottom of the depths of my despair, I cried out to something, someone, anyone who would listen. In a small whimper, I said, "Help me. Please, help me."

But there was no one else in that cell to hear me. Though now I know He heard my plea, I did not understand that at that moment, nor would I until years later.

This was where my journey began. My journey toward redemption.

I knew Hector Delphi had already talked to the President of the Border Brothers. So, I passed a message to a friend of mine. It said, "Get word to these guys. Tell them I've got no problem. It was a mistake on their part, but I want them to know that they were idiots. I've lost everything. I'm facing twenty-five years, and I have never ratted. So why in the hell would I tell somebody about their damn hooch? You tell them I'm coming out and ask them if there is going to be a problem."

When I heard back from my friend that everything was cool, I talked to the police lieutenant running the case. "There was nothing to it," I said, "I feel very confident going back out into the compound."

After being in the Hole for about a week, they let me back into a pod of forty guys until another cell became available. I had no further problems with the Mexican gangbangers.

CHAPTER THIRTY-SIX

Reversal of Fortune

"We've got to attack the New Mexico state conviction,
and if we can overturn it,
your career criminal status will be gone."

—— **Attorney Nancy Hollander**

MY MOTHER ASKED a local Sulphur Springs attorney, Ron Lucas, to request that I be granted clemency by the then Governor of New Mexico, Gary E. Johnson. Ron Lucas, who had represented the family business, both the funeral home and the furniture store, had become a close confidant to my mother concerning affairs about me. In September 1999, the attorney submitted the following letter:

> *At the behest of Diane Emerson, whose son, Jay Emerson, has been imprisoned for the past thirteen years, I ask your consideration in releasing him from confinement.*
>
> *His mother is in her sixties, living alone, and in poor health. She manages a small family business (a funeral home in her family for many years). Still, it is doubtful that she will be able to participate personally much longer. Jay Emerson can and would provide care and attention to his mother and the business as needed. He is deeply aware of what his past actions have cost her, and his love and concern for her will be a formidable deterrent to any repetition of his past errors.*

Jay Emerson has been a well-behaved inmate. He has become a highly qualified craftsman and an artist of outstanding merit. Jay has demonstrated imagination, ingenuity, and dedication to producing major good works in his limited circumstances. I have seen several model historical sailing boats he built to exact scale and detail. He and his mother hope he can pursue a business using these skills to support himself.

Ron R. Lucas, Attorney at Law

Several others wrote similar letters to the judge. Unfortunately, despite these letters' eloquence, passion, and logic, the Governor declined to grant clemency to me.

Federal Pell Grants usually were awarded only to undergraduate students who displayed exceptional financial need and had not yet earned an undergraduate, graduate, doctoral, or professional degree. Pell Grants had been an excellent opportunity for convicted felons to rehabilitate themselves and have an avenue to learn a trade. Pell Grants would pay for it, and colleges would come in and teach them. That is the best thing you can do for a man – educate him and empower him to do something with his life. But at the time, the budget problems in Washington were scattered, and the government felt they had enough people on the streets who needed Pell Grants. So, they began to question why they were awarding them to inmates. Consequently, the government changed the rules to make people incarcerated in a Federal or state penal institution ineligible for a Pell Grant.

But, while the Pell Grants were available, I took every course I could, including automotive and computer technology. I even went to Blackstone School of Law and earned a paralegal degree.

Eventually, I became eligible to move to a minimum security camp. I requested that I be sent to the Federal Prison Camp Eglin, at Eglin Air Force Base in Florida, because they had a Marine Diesel course I wanted to take.

"But you have no family there," they said.

"This is not about family, man. It's about education. Education is where I'm going. You've seen what I've done for the last six years. I want to go to Marine Diesel School. That is where I want to go and what I want to do."

In connection with my request, they scheduled a Team Review with my Unit Manager, Unit Case Manager, and Unit Counselor. My Automotive Vocational Training Instructor and the Vocational Training Coordinator submitted letters to the Review Team in May 2000, similar to this.

> *In anticipation of Inmate Emerson's (11699-077) upcoming Team Review, I am writing to say he is among the best students/workers I have ever had. Mister Emerson has progressed through the curriculum to the advanced stages and greatly assists me mechanically and as a tutor to other students. In addition, his cheerful and optimistic personality, willingness and ability to accept responsibility, and determined attitude make him an invaluable asset to my class.*

As helpful as those letters may have been, a lot happened before my transfer could come about.

My uncle, W.H. 'Bud' Emerson, lived in the affluent residential neighborhood of Pacific Palisades, twenty miles west of downtown Los Angeles. He was well-known within the Hollywood crowd and knew all the directors, producers, and other moviemakers, as well as everybody who was anybody in Hollywood and Sunset Strip. He owned a nightclub called The Crescendo Club, a West Hollywood jazz venue on Sunset Boulevard. I met Bill Cosby there once. Lester Flatt, Earl Scruggs, and the Foggy Mountain Boys played there, and my uncle introduced me to all of them. Even Jerry Lewis was a personal friend of my uncle. Uncle Bud was also a member of the Santa Monica mounted police.

While I was in prison for my Memphis conviction, Bud died. The first responders presumed he had a heart attack while driving his motorhome with his wife. As a result, he drove the vehicle up onto the side of a canyon, tipping it over on its side and leaving my uncle and his wife unconscious. Then, the motorhome caught fire and immolated them both.

Uncle Bud died having no children, but he had established a family trust for the benefit of the Emerson family so his estate would go to his brothers and sisters. However, all of Bud Emerson's brothers and sisters, including my dad, were already deceased, so the money came to the children as secondary beneficiaries. My brother, sister, and I split a fair amount of money.

So, I started playing the stock market, particularly in telecommunications and biomedical companies, and fortunately, I made a little money. Thereafter, some of the guards enjoyed my 'words of wisdom' from a convict. Oh, the irony!

I had heard rumors from Buck that our New Mexico cocaine convictions might be invalid because the search warrant was illegal. We had pleaded guilty to possessing ten ounces of cocaine. So, with the money I inherited from my Uncle Bud, I hired two lawyers, including Attorney Nancy Hollander, who was quite well-known in the Albuquerque area. She referred me to Attorney Gary Mitchell, also from New Mexico.

Nancy Hollander said, "We've got to attack the New Mexico state conviction, and if we can overturn it, your career criminal status will be gone. Then I could file a writ of habeas corpus with the Federal judge, and we should be able to get you out on that."

So, I hired her, and she ran the whole show.

Attorney Gary Mitchell was a white boy who had spent twenty years in the Louisiana State Penitentiary in Angola. That is an unheard-of feat. Nevertheless, in New Mexico, it seems you can have a prior conviction and still get your state license to practice law.

I did not know about Gary's past before. However, his sleeve crept up during one of our meetings, and I saw the tattoos. I asked him about it, and that is when I found out he had been in Angola. I said, "I love you, man, because you've been there. I know I could find no man to fight harder for me than you."

And so, he did.

Of course, earlier in the year, Buck had wanted to represent himself. Even if he had a lawyer, he would try to tell the lawyer what to do. But, as the old adage says, 'he who represents himself has a fool for a client.'

In reality, inmates have only one or two chances to overturn a conviction before 'exhausting all their remedies.'

Buck argued in his petition that the state did not have a search warrant when they arrested us. We had sat for forty minutes in a motel room while the police got a search warrant, but they had already been through the room and found the cocaine. So, they were just trying to cover their bases after the fact. Any evidence thus illegally discovered should be inadmissible under the 'Fruit of the Poisonous Tree' law. He lost, of course, on all points and his conviction was upheld.

In my petition, five specific points served as the basis for my attack on the conviction. By then, I had already served eight years of my sentence and fought this New Mexico conviction for the last four years before I could finally get in front of a judge who would hear my case.

The first judge had been my original sentencing judge. My attorney called the judge as a witness, which precluded him from being my judge, so I had to wait for another judge to be assigned. But by the time my case got to him, the second judge had died of natural causes. So, then, it took a year to find a third judge.

Finally, I had my day in court, and my attorneys started to present their arguments. Attorney Gary Mitchell, my Angola lawyer, mentioned a confidential informant who was integral to the case, Terry Hunter.

"STOP!" the judge shouted.

He called both lawyers forward to the bench. After three minutes or so of discussion with the judge, the lawyers returned and sat down. The judge said, "Mister Emerson, I must stop the proceedings where we are. I'm sorry, but you must find another judge to hear your case."

I sat there dumbfounded. You just can't imagine the 'hoops' you have to go through just to travel to New Mexico from Federal custody in Texas. And now, it was all to no avail.

As it turned out, before he was a judge, he had been the attorney for Terry Hunter, the confidential informant whom this judge and former attorney had convinced to testify against us.

"I know you have been trying to get before the court for a long time," the judge said, "and I will make it a point to get you back up here as quickly as possible."

Six months later, I was back in court before the judge who had heard Buck Cameron's case a year earlier. The judge had denied all of Buck's points. Four of my five points were the same ones Buck had used unsuccessfully. *And I got this guy?! Fuck! I'm doomed again by Buck and his actions.*

This time would be my only chance to be heard, and I got the same judge that denied Buck four of my five arguments! And then, all my remedies would be exhausted. *Oh, God!*

So, I was in court again with the new judge, my lawyer, and five other convicted felons. Everyone's lawyers were there, and the court tried to run through all the dockets quickly.

When the judge heard the case, I thought, *This is going to be rough.*

One of the prosecution lawyers stood up and started talking about some character who was in the courtroom. I didn't know whom he was talking about. And to hear this attorney's words, that person was clearly a horrible man. So, I listened as he ripped into this character, who clearly was despicable and deserved to be in jail for a long time.

Then the attorney pointed at me, and my mind screamed, *No! It's not me! That's not who I am!*

Then I realized, *Wow. That guy was talking about me.*

But that was really me. *Really? Oh, my God!*

And I knew that everything he had said was true.

That character clearly needed to be in jail. But that was not me; that was not who I was, at least in my own mind.

My mother sat behind me in the gallery. She had been there faithfully every day of the hearing. She had gotten herself from Sulphur Springs to Ruidoso by driving six hundred-fifty miles over ten hours. During the break, I said, "I'm sorry, Mama. I know you drove all this way. I'll see you next week at visitation when I get back to prison."

My lawyers testified about 'ineffective assistance of counsel.' One accused attorney said, "Yes, I may have messed up a little since I did not do that."

A rule of life for old school convicts was that you never rat. That was the deal. You stood up to whatever it was. Good lawyers did not want to deal with rats. The accused attorney was a lawyer from New Mexico and was really old school. He knew that we, too, were old school, so he never even came to us and asked if we wanted to rat out. Instead, he tried to get us the best deal he could. In a case precedent, the court found a lawyer to be ineffective assistance of counsel because he never at least tried to bargain with his client.

This attorney confessed to never having allowed us to rat. "Yeah, I never offered it to them because these guys were old school. I knew they wouldn't rat, so I never put that option on the table."

All the while this hearing was going on, I had a severe ear infection and could not hear anything. The Federal health system was pretty pathetic. My ear infection had followed me to this

Lincoln County Jail. I tell you; I was miserable. Absolutely miserable.

The judge summarized his findings by saying, "As to point number one, I thought you guys did great. I think you did very well. I've never heard it approached that way, but I will rule against it. Point number two…"

He went down the line, spending about fifteen seconds on each of the first four points before saying, "But I will rule against it." I could only imagine that this was the same rhetoric Buck had heard just six months before, and was now being repeated for my benefit.

After the fifth point, he talked for about three minutes. I could not hear what he was saying. I looked at my lawyer, and he looked at me. Then the prosecutor stood up and said, "Well, Your Honor, you know we don't have that anymore. So, it's not going to happen."

"What?"

My attorney looked at me and said, "You're free."

"What?"

The prosecutor was going nuts. "Well, you know, we don't have that anymore. We can't do that."

So, the judge said, "You have thirty days to come up with an IRS indictment for Mister Emerson."

"But we can't do that. With what you just ruled, all the evidence is gone. There's nothing we can do."

My attorney looked at me again and said, "You're free."

My fifth point related to the requirements for a confidential informant to testify. To be qualified, a confidential informant must abide by specific guidelines. Terry Hunter never met any of those guidelines.

Terry's handlers should have stripped him to ensure he had no other drugs on him besides the gram of cocaine he bought from Buck and me. Additionally, his handlers never marked the hundred-dollar bill he used to purchase the cocaine.

Since the state failed to qualify Terry Hunter as a confidential informant properly, the court threw out every piece of testimony he had provided, including the cocaine, which was the basis of the whole case.

The state's case was gone.

My attorney looked at me, put his hand on my shoulder, and said quietly, "Congratulations."

At that moment, I dropped my head and whispered, "Ah! So, this is when the dove sings." I finally realized that must be what the Pastor at the revival in Longview in 1960 had meant by that strange expression all those years ago. I never understood that until now.

God had heard my plea in that hellacious dungeon of a cell, and He had saved me. He saved my life and saved my soul. He rescued me out of the belly of the beast.

Praise God! Thank you, Jesus!

After that, I cried for three days whenever I tried to talk to anyone.

After the hearing, a driver picked me up and drove me from New Mexico back to Three Rivers in Texas, with my hands cuffed behind my back the whole time. After the ten-hour, six hundred seventy-mile trip, my wrists were *so* sore. When we arrived, I begged for aspirin to reduce the pain.

After the reversal of my second conviction in New Mexico, the court no longer classified me as a career criminal with three federal drug convictions. So, six months after my return to prison, my attorney filed a 'writ of habeas corpus' under the Federal court's jurisdiction to reevaluate my case and re-sentence me. A writ of habeas corpus (literally meaning to 'produce the body') is a court order demanding that a public official deliver an imprisoned individual to the court and show a valid reason for that person's continued detention.

Since I was in a maximum security prison but no longer classified as a maximum security inmate, the law held the Federal government liable for my person every day I was there. So, they were anxious to get my case handled. They had me before the original Federal judge and the prosecuting attorney in six months, while other inmates waited years to have their cases adjudicated.

The original prosecuting attorney, Timothy R. DiSenza, had retired and became a specialist in white-collar computer crime. He no longer handled drug cases, but they pulled him back in any way. I sat in front of them, and they reviewed my case and history.

When they finished their review, I offered, "In all my time in prison, I never had an incident report. I didn't stab nobody, and nobody stabbed me."

The prosecuting attorney said, "Your honor, I have no problem releasing this man."

The judge looked at me in my prison clothes and said, "As far as I'm concerned, with these sentencing guidelines, you have served your time. So, Mister Emerson, you go to that cage over there. I will have the U.S. Marshals draw up your release papers, and in forty-five minutes, you can go home."

Oh, my God! I broke down on the spot. I didn't care that other men, hardened convicts, would see me cry. I was sure they would do the same. I couldn't have stopped myself anyway. I wailed uncontrollably for pretty much another three days. I swear, I couldn't even talk. I stuttered and choked, and then came the tears.

I flew home on Friday, May 11, 2001, in my prison clothes on Southwest Airlines with my lawyer. I genuinely believe that was the day I was physically reborn. Right there on that airplane.

Yet, I still faced ten years of supervised probation, which was unheard of. Usually, you get out about halfway, and then they say, "You've been a good boy, so we'll cut you loose now." But I served out my probation day for day, for ten whole years. Long ago, I had paid the twenty-five-thousand-dollar fine out of my inheritance from Uncle Bud.

I was thirty years old when I went to prison for the first time, and I left prison for the last time at the age of forty-eight. I had spent almost fourteen of those eighteen years incarcerated. About one-third of my life. What a waste. What a fuckin' waste.

Act Four

REDEEMING
INMATE 11699-077

Chapter Thirty-Seven

Just As I Am

"Just as I am, without one plea
But that Thy blood was shed for me
And that Thou bid'st me come to Thee
Oh, Lamb of God, I come, I come!"

—— **Charlotte Elliot**
Just As I Am

I MET MY MOTHER at DFW Airport, and that was when I first truly knew I had emerged out of the belly of the beast. During my prison years, I had been in a state of suspended animation the whole time. Now I was free! FREE! **FREE!**

I returned to my mother's house in Sulfur Springs, where I stayed for two years until she retired from the funeral home business.

Within three days of my arrival back home, I called an old girlfriend, Dixie, off whose breasts I used to snort cocaine. By then, she had been married and divorced and had a six-year-old daughter.

"Hi! Do you know who this is?" I asked.

"Yeah, I know who this is, but it can't be because you ain't supposed to be out for another nine years."

"Well, I'm out now, and I got home yesterday. If you want, I would like to meet you for dinner."

We met for dinner, she brought her daughter, and we picked up right where we had left off.

Dixie reintroduced me to civilized society. I had been away from society and American culture for the last twelve years, and so many things had changed in the meantime. Dixie taught me how to operate a gas pump using a credit card. Who had a credit card? She took care of me, worshiped me, and loved me. And, of course, I treated her like shit. Frankly, I didn't know anything else.

Her father was a Sunday School teacher, and her mother played the piano at the Central Baptist Church in Sulphur Springs. Since I had dated their daughter before I went to prison, they knew everything about me. Understandably, they were somewhat concerned about me taking their daughter out again. So, to assuage their fears, I started worshipping with Dixie at her parents' church.

When I was in prison, I read the Bible many times, but I didn't understand it. I tried to read it, absorb it, and see what it was saying, but it just didn't click for me. There were guys in prison who purported to be Christians, but as soon as they got out and walked past that last door, they threw that Good Book right in the trash can.

I have always been a religious person of one kind or another. My parents would drop us off at church on Sunday, but they never went themselves. Sunday School was important, and I cared about the church and spirituality. But I hated the church members' hypocrisy and cynicism, so I just threw it away. I rejected the Christian church.

Before going to prison, I turned to Buddhism. I loved Buddhism and Hinduism. They were inclusive, they loved everybody, and everyone was going to heaven. I believed we were all looking at the same God; there were just different ways of getting up the mountain. So, before I started smuggling full-time and getting caught up in the 'Dharma,' or divine law of Buddhism and Hinduism, I became a Sikh for a couple of years. I grew my hair long, wore a turban, eschewed leather, and lived as a vegetarian. I got up at four in the morning, took cold showers, and honed myself. I thought that was getting me closer to God. I won't say it was, but I didn't understand it was actually taking me away from the One True God.

I created my own religion. I took what I liked from this one, what I liked from that one. That's good, I'll take that. I don't like that, so I'll cut that out. I ended up fabricating my own religion and working with that. Oh yeah, let's add a little meditation and prayer. We'll even fold our hands like Christians. But it was still me, my self-effort, my created religion, me doing my own thing. It was not real and not valid.

However, after about four months of listening and learning in Dixie's church, I became challenged by this new world I was discovering. Now that I had the benefit of a little guidance understanding the words of the Bible I was reading, things began to make more and more sense. Eventually, it became clear to me what I needed to do.

So, one Sunday, during the altar call at the end of the service, while Dixie's mother played the piano and everyone in the congregation sang, *Just As I Am*, I went forward and made my profession of faith. In prayer, I verbally gave myself over to God.

One of the church elders took me to a back room, where I answered all his questions. Then, he pronounced me saved and took me back into the sanctuary to stand before the congregation.

But truthfully, I really did not understand what I was doing at that point.

I had surprised everyone. When Dixie's mother saw me going forward, she whispered, "What the hell is he doing now?"

I had publicly made my verbal commitment to Jesus Christ, but I still had not yet fully changed. Instead, I had just begun the process. The elder explained that I was in a state of 'prevenient grace,' which was a 'divine grace' that operates on the human will before it genuinely turns to God. He would start showing His love to me at a certain moment in my lifetime.

However, for now, I was 'justified,' meaning I had demonstrated a just, right, or reasonable basis for being declared righteous and worthy of salvation. Presently, I was being 'sanctified' as I would grow in 'righteousness' and be freed from guilt and sin.

In short, I had stated my belief in Jesus Christ, confessed my sinful nature, and declared Him to be my Lord and Savior. In return, God had forgiven my sins and promised me eternal life in Heaven. I know that sounds like a lot of Christian lingo, but basically, this is the process that would lead me to becoming a new creation in Christ. My responsibility would be to worship Him and follow and obey His commands.

A week later, I asked the pastor to baptize me by full immersion. My mother had me baptized in the Methodist church as a child, but I thought, *Well, hell, let's just go ahead and do it all.*

I said to the pastor, "Let's do it next week."

"Great!" he said, "April 15 – Easter Sunday. Couldn't be better."

"What?" I did not fathom the significance of that.

My mother was a diehard Methodist, a Methodist-Buddhist, in fact. She had always held the Baptists in great disdain. Her father had taught her that the ruination of Sulphur Springs would be because of the termites and the Baptists. So, my mother was not really happy about me dating a Baptist girl.

I told my mother, "I've got something significant happening to me next week, and I'd appreciate it if you would be there."

"Of course, honey. I'd love to be there. What is it?"

"Well, I'm getting baptized in the Baptist church."

"Oh, FUCK!"

I had never heard my mother use that word.

We were in public at the time, so I said, "Well, I'm damn glad I didn't tell you this in the privacy of our home."

"If you think I'm going to go down there to shake their Baptist hands first thing in the morning, you've got another thing coming," she said with both a wry and disdainful smile at the same time.

"I'm not expecting you to do anything. I'm just letting you know this is what I'm doing."

On Easter Sunday, my mother showed up at the church after all. She sat on the back pew and watched my baptism incognito.

After the service, she said, "I was not going to go down in front and stand there and shake all their Baptist hands."

"Yes, ma'am."

But after that, I could feel my faith start to grow.

Dixie's father was an excellent teacher. He had studied the Bible extensively, favoring the books of Paul over the Gospel of Luke, and he loved the Book of Romans.

We had some great conversations, challenging each other on various topics. He wanted me to stay in Sulphur Springs and marry his daughter. He wanted me to be a part of their family.

I said, "I want to become a boatbuilder. I've got this desire to go to the Pacific Northwest. I want to build boats, and there is a school there that I want to attend."

He paused for a moment and then said, "Is that what God wants? Or what you want?"

I might ask him the same.

CHAPTER THIRTY-EIGHT

GQ Dude

"My brother and I stopped
seeing each other after that."

—— **Jay Emerson**

WHEN I RETURNED HOME FROM PRISON, I started working in the family business as the Office Manager of Tanner Furniture and Funeral Home. By then, my mother and my half-brother Mike had become co-owners of the company. My mother was the President, and Mike was the General Manager.

To all outward appearances, Mike was about as 'GQ' *(Gentleman's Quarterly)* in style as you could be within the Sulphur Springs Chamber of Commerce and the general community. Being very high GQ, Mike would have done fine if he operated in Dallas, selling to doctors, lawyers, and corporate businessmen. But we were in Sulfur Springs, the dairy capital of Hopkins County in East Texas. Mike was extravagant by local standards and simply not doing it right. He just didn't fit into the local community culture. He wanted to be somewhere else. Of course, the funeral home tied itself closely to the local churches.

But Mike was going through some tough times because he had become addicted to methamphetamine. He kept this secret from everybody except me because I knew my brother. A 'friend' of his had gotten him into it. Mike was shooting meth into his legs and in between his toes.

Additionally, he was snorting coke and consequently created a deviated septum in his nose. Cocaine ruins your nose. I know that from personal experience. In this condition, he was destroying the family business, and ruining everything.

In my absence, while I was in prison, Mike had run most of the Tanner business into the ground, causing the company to shut its doors. So, our mother moved him over to the funeral home on a supervised basis, and he promptly began ruining that business as well.

Consequently, after my release, I talked my mother into selling the business and enjoying the fruits of her labor while she still could. None of the grandkids wanted to come into the business, and if she were to die and my brother were to take the business, none of us would ever see a nickel from that company.

Ultimately, my mother agreed to sell the business, which spoiled everything for Mike.

So, we offered to sell our share of the business to him.

"We will offer it to you for a certain amount, which we think is fair for everyone," our mother said.

"No, that's too much," Mike responded. "I'm not gonna pay that."

I reminded him, "This is our mother's retirement, medical, and everything from now on. This is what it's worth, this is what she needs, and she's giving you a discount at that."

"Well, I ain't gonna do it," he said.

My brother never came to visit me in prison, so he really didn't know that I had prepared my way to understand business, including earning a paralegal degree. Besides, I already had the worldly common sense that the University of Hard Knocks can provide. I was no dummy as to the destructive business nature he possessed while under the influence of drugs. I know, I've been there too.

So, I found somebody else, and I sold the business to them and made fifty thousand dollars in the process. Mike also made fifty thousand dollars just because Mom gave him the money.

"I can't believe you've been here just six months, Jay, and I've been here for more than thirty years, and still, you made as much as me."

My brother and I stopped seeing each other after that.

CHAPTER THIRTY-NINE

A Woman of Substance

"A good woman is the loveliest flower
that blooms under heaven;
and we look with love and wonder
upon its silent grace, its pure fragrance,
its delicate bloom of beauty."

—— **William Makepeace Thackeray**

IN RETROSPECT, I owe great apologies to, and need much forgiveness from, the women who passed through my life over the years. It would be an understatement to say I did not treat them well. From the time I was thirty years old until I was forty-eight, I spent all but four of those years in prison. Unfortunately, the prison system offered no formal or informal training classes about the proper etiquette for dealing with women. On the contrary, male convicts typically treated women with great disrespect and condescension.

Consequently, I was insensitive and dismissive of women. I offered only the minimal level of gentleness and affection without truly understanding the emotions and mentality of women or the proper rules of engagement.

These women to whom I refer included my first wife, Kim, and girlfriends Dixie and Brit. But most importantly, Paula Jean, aka 'PJ,' who has been the best and whom I treated the worst.

I was anxious to build my first full-size boat, and I decided to make a wooden canoe. I needed a workplace, so I reopened the Tanner Furniture Store doors while Mike still ran the funeral business across the street. The floor-to-ceiling windows running the entire width of the building let in some beautiful light. So, that became my shop. People driving down Gilmer Street at night could see me through the windows working on my canoe. I usually went there at about four in the afternoon and stayed until eleven at night.

After about four months of labor, I proudly displayed some of the fruits of my efforts in the windows, a beautifully handcrafted western red cedar canoe, and several of the model sailing ships I had built in prison. People would stop and watch me work through the windows and sometimes come in to visit.

Building the model boats in prison taught me construction techniques and gave me an idea of what's involved in boat building. I learned how to work with wood, the purpose of certain parts, and some obstacles I might encounter building a real boat. Building the canoe was just another step in the process of realizing my dream. It was the first actual application of my skills.

I knew that, obviously, I couldn't sail around the world in this canoe, but at least, I hoped to market some of my work to generate the funding needed to fulfill that dream.

Jerry Kitchens was one of my hang gliding friends, and I had become a silent partner in his business. In the early days of flying planes across the border, it was 'birds of a feather stick together.' So, this was a way to get into the flying community back then.

Then, after I left for prison, Jerry got involved in a drone program with the Pentagon, where he held a high-level security clearance. In those days, drones were called 'Remote Pilotless Vehicles' or 'RPVs'. Jerry once served as a consultant to the Pentagon on an archeological program that employed RPVs to search for Noah's Ark on Mt. Ararat.

Jerry was also a paranoid schizophrenic. He was one of the only people I knew who took Elavil® and Librium® together. Elavil is a tricyclic antidepressant, and Librium is an antianxiety agent. The two drugs combined treat mental depression with anxiety or nervous tension. I tried it once. When I woke up three days later, Cousin Buck was on the phone, "Where the hell are you, man? You got a car with drugs in it. And we don't know where you are."

"Well, I'm just now waking up."

I had taken only a half dose. Jerry ate them like M&Ms.®

One time, a group of black men gave Jerry a major beatdown. After that, he swore to God that he would never again take a beating like that. So, he started carrying handguns, three at a time, two on his waist and one on his ankle. Just consider for a minute the possible outcomes of an angry, mentally unstable person carrying not just one gun but multiple guns.

After I had left prison and then returned to Sulphur Springs, Jerry lived in Quitman, the next little town over, about twenty-five miles south. Quitman had an airport where we kept a hangar to store all our old memorabilia.

Jerry wanted to help me get re-established. He was an entrepreneur and tried to give me ideas about things I could do. As part of that process, he wanted me to meet a woman he planned to marry, which surprised me because I had never known him to date anyone. It was not that he was gay; it was just that he was really into whatever he was doing and had no time for women.

"Well, far out, man! I'm proud of you," I said, shaking his hand. "Yeah, I'll be happy to meet her."

Back when Mike had run the furniture business into the ground, we just shut and locked the doors and never went back in. So, subsequently, I held three garage sales to dispose of the leftover clutter. In the third sale, I also sold some of my own personal property.

Jerry came to the first garage sale and brought his fiancé, Paula Jean Goodner, or 'PJ,' as he called her. She and I immediately discovered we were both big huggers, so we enthusiastically engaged in one of our mutually favorite practices when Jerry introduced us.

Wanting to ingratiate myself with my friend's fiancé, I acted like, 'she be running things,' and so let her in on things that were happening.

William Winchester, Jerry, and I had planned a weekend road trip to the Texas coast, so I asked PJ, "Do you mind if Jerry comes with us to South Padre Island to hang out with the boys?"

"No. I don't care what Jerry does."

I thought, *Wow! This chick is cool!*

I was selling an old futon mattress that had been collecting dust for twelve years and had a big blood stain on it. PJ decided she wanted it, but Jerry couldn't carry it home for her in his vehicle.

"Do you mind if I deliver it to her, Jerry?" I asked. "I'll take it to Dallas. It'll give me an excuse to go to a good restaurant." In those days, you could go through every restaurant in Sulphur Springs in about two weeks.

Jerry was agreeable to that plan, so a week later, PJ and I met in a parking lot in Oak Lawn near her apartment. We sat in my truck and talked for more than four hours. During the course of our conversation, I learned that her brother, Jim Goodner, had died of lung cancer in the Oklahoma State Penitentiary in McAlester, where he had been sentenced for possessing marijuana with intent to distribute. Jim had sheltered his sister from that aspect of his life.

And now she was sitting with someone who had been in prison, too, and she was peppering me with questions, trying to gain an understanding of her brother's life. Those four hours went by so fast, and they were my first really relevant, heart-to-heart talk with a person I respected.

In years past, Jerry lived in a frat house at Southeastern Oklahoma State University in Durant. One day the frat house President said to him, "Hey, man, we need some pot. Why don't you go see your friend in Texas? You can get it cheap from him. Bring it back here, and we can sell whatever you can get to our friends."

So, Jerry came to Texas, I sold him some pot, and he took it back to the university.

It turned out that the frat house President was PJ's brother, Jim, who later died in prison.

As we sat talking in my truck, I said, "This is the first time I've had an intelligent conversation with anyone in twelve years."

"Really?"

It was now three o'clock in the morning. "Yeah. Hey, I'm hungry. Let's go get some dinner."

So, I took her to a local restaurant called Lucky's Café on Oak Lawn Avenue near Lemmon Avenue. Lucky's was a well-known everyday family café with windows all around, a checkerboard floor, and mid-century metal tables and chairs. The restaurant was operated by gay men and was frequented by gay diners. It was not unusual to see two men in a booth engaging in a serious 'lip lock.' Of course, this was nothing to me since I had seen a lot worse in prison, offered freely or taken painfully, your choice.

We arrived in the early morning hour, when only a few other customers were still there. We sat in a booth that afforded us at least a modicum of privacy. Over dinner, we held an easy and free-flowing conversation. We learned that PJ had a degree in art and never threw anything away because she believed she could convert it to an art piece, and I had plenty of junk I was going to throw out.

After that, PJ came to my shop two more times, even though it was an eighty-mile drive from Oak Lawn to Sulphur Springs. The first time she came back, she brought her dad, who was enthralled with the canoe I was building. The second time, she brought her daughter and told me she wanted to buy the canoe for her father.

In short order, PJ's and my attraction for each other grew well beyond our mutual affinity for hugging. Consequently, the following conversation ensued.

"Well, shit! I am a rotten bastard, a snake. I snaked my best friend. I feel terrible about what I did," I told PJ.

"Why?" she asked.

"Because you and Jerry are getting married."

"What?!"

"I snaked my best friend, you know? Screwed his fiancé."

"I am not his fiancé, and we certainly are not getting married."

"You're not?"

"Oh, hell no," she said. "Let me tell you. When my brother died in prison, Jerry contacted my family to offer his condolences because he and Jim had been friends in the fraternity. However, my mother refused to talk to him because she knew of Jerry's involvement with Jim's drug activities. She sent me to talk to him instead. He asked me how he could reach Jim's widow, Connie. I thought that was a little creepy, so I refused to help him. Then I told him never to come back to my house again."

"And did he stay away?"

"No! He came back two or three times. After that, I realized he was more than just a little strange."

I spent that night with PJ. I left at seven-thirty in the morning, and Jerry called me by ten o'clock.

"Hey, buddy, what's going on? Where you been, and what'chu been doing?" he asked. Before I could answer, he said, "Well, guess what. I know where you been, what you been doing, and who you been doing."

"Oh? How so?"

"Maybe you didn't know, Jay, but I had a private investigator following PJ."

"Really? How come?"

"Well, she was involved in a road rage incident a week ago, and I thought she needed protection. But never mind that. So, listen up. If I ever see you again, *I will kill you. Don't even come on my property.*"

I called PJ and told her what had happened.

"Oh, he doesn't know anything," she said.

"Yes, I think he does. He had a private investigator following you."

"Oh, bullshit."

"I think he did because, by ten o'clock this morning, he already knew what we were doing."

PJ and I continued dating, and Jerry continued threatening.

One day, under the windshield wiper of my truck, I found an envelope with a note scribbled on it.

I'm killing your fuckin' ass.

You better be moved out and far away before I return.

Your Old Cellie

None of my 'old cellies' wrote this note. Jerry Kitchens wrote this note.

CHAPTER FORTY

An Insufferable Ladies' Man

"As I was fighting for you,
I realized I was fighting to be lied to,
fighting to be taken for granted,
fighting to be disappointed,
and fighting to be hurt again.
So, I started fighting to let go."

—— **Bernard King Stephens, Jr.**

HAVING SOLD THE BUSINESS, I took my mother up to the Pacific Northwest to live out the last of her days in relative peace and ease. My brother stayed in Sulphur Springs and ran the business for the new owners for a year until they laid him off. That was our agreement. They had to keep him for a year so he would have time to figure out what he wanted to do. Then, if he didn't perform after a year, they could do whatever they wanted with him.

PJ and I had been dating for a couple of years, and then I went off to Washington State to attend boatbuilding school. While she was sad for me to leave, she also knew I was trying to make myself a better man by attending boatbuilding school in the Northwest. And she planned to visit periodically.

PJ was fully aware that I was a shameless womanizer. There were three other women in Sulphur Springs with whom I occasionally 'consorted.' PJ knew about these women because I told her. Or maybe she weaseled it out of me. I'm not sure. At any rate, she knew that these were some of the demons I was dealing with. Unfortunately, when I went to Washington, I took all my old behaviors concerning women with me to continue them up there.

In Washington, I fooled around with three other women. One of them, Brit, was twenty-six years old, roughly half my age. She had long blonde hair down to her waist. While the sex may have been great, our age difference complicated maintaining a satisfying relationship. We had nothing in common, except for sex and occasional drugs. Brit enjoyed doing evaluations and reports for newly developed sex toys, so there really was nothing to talk about. We didn't like the same music, and her friends were too young for me.

The first time PJ visited me, I picked her up at Seattle-Tacoma International Airport and then drove a hundred-miles in two-hours to Port Townsend. When we got to the turn-off for my house at Kala Point, I kept going straight because I wanted to go into town.

I turned to PJ and said, "You understand, right? I won't ever have a friend I don't sleep with."

[Silence and PJ looking straight ahead.]

I could tell that bothered her, but she said nothing at that time.

We went to dinner, and unexpectedly, Brit entered the restaurant and sat at our table. She immediately started talking about me having sex with one of her friends.

Brit looked at PJ and said, "But I told the girl it doesn't matter who Jay has sex with. He can have sex with anyone he wants."

Brit was talking about that in front of PJ, but in my naiveté about male-female relationships, I thought nothing of it.

Then she looked at PJ and asked, "Are you a Christian?"

PJ said, "Yes."

It seemed a strange question and not one to end a conversation on. But off Brit went, as if she had finished her business and now had someplace to go.

It must have been evident to PJ that something was going on because she knew Brit had been in my house and texted me all the time.

We arrived at the house that evening, and I was in the bedroom, and PJ was in the kitchen. With tears streaming down her face, she asked, "Why did you have me come here? Why? I want you to tell me why, right now!"

Her question caught me off-guard. I was mystified. *What was her problem? Why was this woman crying? Why was she doing this?*

Then, as I stood there, dumbfounded, not knowing what to do, the light in my head went on. It was a revelation, just like when I read that first issue of *WoodenBoat* magazine.

Something like this might normally take a long time for someone to realize, but I saw and realized it immediately in this case. And I knew I had to act upon it.

CHAPTER FORTY-ONE

The Proposal

"That might earn me a swift kick in the balls."

—— **Jay Emerson**

FOR MOST PEOPLE, there are only one or two people who ever come into your life that are supposed to stay there forever. And, at that moment, I realized PJ was one of them. She was a true woman of substance. So, my Spirit told me in a very distinct voice, "Don't blow this one, Jay."

And at that point, while PJ was still crying, I knew I would marry this woman.

So, what should I do now? Should I go over to her, pat her shoulder, and say, "Uh, I'm sorry, baby. I don't suppose you would wanna, uh, get, uh, married, would you? Hmm, maybe not."

That might earn me a swift kick in the balls.

She couldn't wait to get out of there.

So, for three days, I decided I would not tell her even though I knew what I was going to do. I felt a little time for her to cool off couldn't hurt. Timing is everything, I always say.

PJ had called American Airlines to make a reservation to go home early because she didn't want to stay up there with me and my 'friend.'

Knowing she wouldn't want to ride in the car with me all the way to the airport, I called one of my buddies to take her, and she went home.

A few days after she got home, I called her. After a few awkward moments, I said, "PJ, I want to spend my life with you."

She was quiet for a while and then said, "I won't have someone that goes out on me. And I won't have someone that yells at me. And I will have someone that prays with me every day." There were several other conditions also.

And without hesitation, I said, "I can do that. I will do that."

The next day, I told Brit, "I need to tell you something. What I have to say may sound a little weird."

My relationship with Brit had been a tryst, nothing more. Hell, I was as old as her father. The girl's passion was testing sex toys for manufacturers. She was a nymphomaniac, and I was dying every week. I could not keep up with this lady. I was going to die.

"I've asked PJ to marry me," I said.

"You asked her to marry you?"

"Yeah, Brit. I'm sorry, but I chose PJ over you."

I saw Brit once more after that, and I could tell that last statement really hurt her. This was a revelation to me. I saw this girl's countenance fall; her face showed the hurt and pain she felt because of losing to an 'older' woman.

I should have never said that – more of my struggle with learning how to treat women right.

Two days later, I had Brit out in my rowboat. We were still friends. We were not going to have sex, but we were good friends. Like 'friends without benefits,' if you will.

I was rowing us across the bay to have some beers when PJ called. "What are you doing? Why haven't you called?"

And I didn't know the answer to that question. I had asked PJ to marry me. So, I guess I was supposed to call her every day after that. I was utterly devoid of any understanding of relationship rules and etiquette. I didn't know my boundaries or her expectations of me.

"So, what are you doing?" she repeated.

"I'm just sitting here with Brit. What should I be doing?"

"You should call me occasionally to let me know we're really doing this."

"Oh. Okay. I'll start doing that."

Brit was laughing and carrying on in the background. Clearly, that was for PJ's benefit.

"Who did you say you were with?"

"Well, I have Brit here."

[Awkward.]

So, I had to learn how to act and treat PJ because I obviously had no appropriate behavioral skills coming out of prison, where we did not practice such things as social skills and etiquette. I had no understanding of my boundaries and limitations. I missed out on much of my cultural education by being in prison during the years when most young people were learning how to act in society.

And I am still learning my social skills to this day. For example, PJ worked two jobs as a mental health therapist. In the daytime, she worked for Grayson County doing behavior intervention in the schools. She would observe children and develop a plan to help them succeed. These were children with issues too big and complicated for them to handle on their own. Then, she also had her private practice at night and on the weekends. So, she was working six and a half days a week. She would go in at eight in the morning and work until nine-thirty at night. That's about an eighty-eight-hour work week! Like holding down two full-time jobs at the same time.

Whereas I was working only three or four hours a day and taking naps, I didn't see anything wrong with that. After all, it wasn't much different from my prison schedule, which I had followed for the last twelve years. But clearly, I needed more understanding of reasonable expectations. PJ would eventually straighten me out, but it was a long process. I guess we finally worked most things out because we are still together. But I'm sure she would say it was and is still a struggle. And that would be fair. I couldn't argue.

When I took PJ to meet my half-brother Mike for the first time, he met her at the door saying in a none-too-friendly manner, "What are you doing here? I have no family. What are you doing here?"

She said, "Mike, I don't know about the past, but I just want to meet Jay's brother."

And he calmed down then, took us in, and became a regular human being. So, we went out to eat, and he had to be back for a funeral, but he stayed until the last minute and was very friendly the whole time.

PJ and I finally married on December 29, 2004, and she moved to Port Hadlock-Irondale with me. We stayed at my mother's house for a couple of months until we figured out what we wanted to do. Of course, our expectation was that we would stay there.

She had two years left until retirement, but Washington State would not honor any retirement benefits she had accrued through the Teacher Retirement System of Texas, meaning she would have to start all over. I didn't think that was fair, so I told her I would not allow her to do that. "We'll go back to Texas for a couple of years, let you retire, and then come back here."

My mother knew that my destiny was boatbuilding. And if I left Washington and went back to Texas, that would be the end of that dream. But now, another woman was stepping in, caring for her son, leaving my mother thinking PJ was interfering with her perceived rightful role. Of course, PJ was treating me like a king. So, the prospect of our leaving drove a wedge between them.

"I can't go back. I can't go back to Texas," I said. "There is a lot of bad stuff there for me."

That bad stuff being my partners in crime and the whole drug smuggling world I was trying to escape. I knew the old triggers, old habits, and old friends would still be there. I needed to go someplace new and find new friends, new places, and new things, so I wouldn't be influenced to fall back into my old habits and behaviors."

So, my mother was under the impression, "Well, hell, he's going back to Texas again after getting this far? It's like he's taking a step backward."

But it was leaving Texas that saved me. I left my old friends, found new friends, and developed a new mentality, body, and everything else.

CHAPTER FORTY-TWO

Boatbuilding School

"For I know the plans I have for you,"
declares the Lord,
"plans to prosper you and not to harm you,
plans to give you hope and a future."

— **Jeremiah 29:11 (NIV)**

SINCE I FIRST SAW that copy of *WoodenBoat* magazine in FCI Texarkana, I dreamed of building boats. Everything I have done from that moment in the cell looking at that boat on the cover was to fulfill my dream of building wooden models of Gloucester Schooners for collectors on the East Coast. I would read every piece of literature I could find on nautical history and become a member of nautical museums.

After I had been home from prison for about a year, I visited the Northwest School of Wooden Boatbuilding in Port Hadlock, Washington. My visit lasted four hours. Then, I came home, packed all our belongings, and moved my mom and myself up to Portland, Oregon, where my sister Laury lived.

When we sold the family business, I came away with about fifty thousand dollars. I paid off the twenty-five-thousand-dollar debt for my release from prison and then kept twenty-five thousand dollars. I used fifteen thousand for boatbuilding school and ten thousand for living expenses.

At the time, I was still under supervised release. Accordingly, I had to get the approval of my probation officer to relocate. When I told him about my plans, he was immediately in tune with me fulfilling those goals. He was supportive of everything I had done. Additionally, as part of my supervised release, a federal mandate required me to have a place to live before I moved. So, I arrived about four months before school started and began making living arrangements for my mother and myself.

My mother was a creative individual, a talented artist with phenomenal decorating ideas, and Craftsman-style houses were her specialty. By agreement, when we moved to Portland, my mother took the back bedroom of my sister's house.

For myself, I rented a room in a Craftsman bungalow in a gated community in Port Hadlock-Irondale from a lady who was gone eight months out of the year. The rent was four hundred dollars a month with bills paid, and sometimes, I would have to be a gigolo. That wasn't so bad. When you're just out of prison, your standards are pretty low.

Sometimes, when my landlady was not there, I would bring my mother up to visit. On one of these visits, she said, "Let's find a house to buy."

And so, she did, in Port Townsend, about ten miles north. The house had been on the market for less than twenty-four hours when she bought it. She made it a home with her decorating skills and enjoyed it for the last five years of her life. My mother had made it beautiful, including spending twenty thousand dollars landscaping the house.

There was a lot of boatbuilding activity in Portland, and I met a fellow named Pat, who restored monuments, houses, doors, and door pieces. He was also a boat builder, and he let me use his shop to make some repairs to my two-man rowing scull. One day, he said,

"I have friends up there in Port Townsend, and I know about that boatbuilding school."

"Really? What do you know about it?"

"Well, you'll see what I mean when you get up there. I know some people."

I'll see what?

Then, when I was in Port Townsend two months before I started school, I ran into Pat again, and he introduced me to Captain Robert D'Arcy, who was restoring a schooner named *Martha*. Captain D'Arcy was presently building a new deck on the schooner. He was going to remove the old deck and construct a new composite, modern deck on the old boat. So, D'Arcy took me on as his assistant, giving me hands-on training and an extraordinary opportunity to work on a magnificent historic boat.

She was an exceptional boat, and it was an honor for me to have the opportunity to work on her.

Martha was built in 1907 for the Commodore of the San Francisco Yacht Club, J. R. Hanify, and named after his wife, Martha Fitzmaurice Hanify. *Martha* was a B.B. Crowninshield design built at the W.F. Stone Boat Yard in San Francisco. The boat was sixty-eight feet on deck, eighty-four feet sparred, with a sixteen-foot beam and an eight-foot draft. Her planking was fir and silver Bali on oak frames, and her interior was Honduran mahogany, graced with leaded glass cabinetry below decks.

Indeed, she was a gorgeous boat.

She also had an interesting provenance. Legendary Hollywood actor James Cagney owned her from 1934 to 1943. Now, *Martha* is the oldest working sailboat in the state of Washington.

In the meantime, before school started, I worked at the Boat Haven Marina in Port Townsend.

I was freelancing as a 'tailgater' scraping hulls. The brick-and-mortar businesses in the local community hated tailgaters because we worked on their customers' boats and took that business away from them. They couldn't compete with us because we were charging a third of the going rates and living out of our trucks.

Finally, I got a job working on a boat called the *Oz, Tater, and Patty*. The owners used this boat for whale watching in Hawaii. Additionally, whale scientists would bring their equipment and stay on board while they observed the whales. This boat was a fifty-foot yacht used as a liveaboard and chartered out to whale scientists, and they allowed me to come on their craft while I was going to boatbuilding school. I rebuilt their galley and made cabinets and a wet locker for them.

Felix, one of the other guys on the *Oz, Tater, and Patty* was an accomplished boatbuilder. I had my tools from the boatbuilding school, but this guy had no tools at all, and yet he did everything with nothing. He had been doing it all his life and now was about seventy. Felix was an old San Francisco hippie who would go down to his house in Scorpion Bay in Mexico, where he had a Haydite block house, and surf off the beach in the winter. Then, in the summer, he came back to Washington State, where he surfed and hired out to work on boats.

Felix taught me things that made me question the necessity of going to boat school. So, I asked one guy about that, "Hey, man, should I even go to boatbuilding school?"

He said, "You ought to use that fifteen thousand dollars to pay rent and come down here and work in this yard, and you'll learn everything you need to know."

Another guy said, "No, go ahead and go to school. They'll teach you everything you need to know."

And that's what I did. I went to boatbuilding school as planned. But in my spare time while attending school, I hung around at Boat Haven and did some work on my own at their facility.

My first official customer was a retired middle linebacker from the Oakland Raiders who had bought a sixty-foot schooner with no sails and the wrong rigging. But he motored it everywhere he wanted to go. It was a beautiful boat, but he had no idea what to do with it. So, Captain D'Arcy referred him to me.

It was my first paid work, and the guy was what we call a 'putty and paint and make it what it ain't' customer. At first, I was going to do just one little part. Then he asked me if I would do something else. "Yeah, I can do that." And this continued to happen.

Then, when I handed him the bill, he just about shit. I mean, he came unglued. And I thought I was being very fair. I wasn't charging even thirty dollars an hour. He kept adding tasks but never added up the cost.

I billed him about three thousand dollars. Oh, boy! Here was this big black middle linebacker, literally overflowing with muscles. And I was very upset about all this. "Wow, man, what did I do wrong?"

I went to Captain D'Arcy, and he said, "Jay, you're going to have to deal with people like that all your life. This is what happens, and this is how it works. But man, you're only as good as your work."

Ultimately, the linebacker paid me a significantly reduced amount from what I billed him.

"I just ain't going to pay that."

"Man, why can't you?"

"I can, but I ain't. I'll pay this," he said.

Finally, I conceded, "What the hell? Just give me what you will."

That is how I learned about written agreements, change orders, progress payments, and building in cushion for just such cheapskate clients.

Attending the Northwest School of Wooden Boatbuilding in Port Hadlock-Irondale was the happiest time of my life. It was the first time I had ever found a real purpose in my life. The very first time.

The boatbuilding program consisted of four quarters, the first of which began in October. However, because of when I arrived, I took the interior joinery class that would typically start in the summer quarter. So, I was doing the last quarter first. To get permission to do this, I met with the director of the school and the lead instructors to show them the work I had done in Texas. I showed them the canoe I built in Sulphur Springs and some projects I did in prison. And I pointed out that I still had all my fingers. It was enough to convince them to let me start with the summer quarter and then do the other three quarters beginning in the fall.

Most of the students were in their early twenties, with a few even younger, so at fifty-two, I was outside the mean age for the program but still not the oldest. They were an eclectic group of people from around the world. Some were retired professionals, and others were hippies, boat builders from Alaska, or commercial fishermen.

Before coming to the school, I had been standing beside Sulfur Springs funeral home gravesides for three years in a hundred-plus-degree Texas heat, wearing a three-piece suit and just dying. I couldn't wait for the cold weather of the Northwest, and I loved and absorbed it. I grew a long beard and wore Carhartt jackets. It was very pleasant, and I enjoyed it more than I could ever explain.

My first project was to build a toolbox to hold the thousand dollars' worth of tools I had to buy. Additionally, I had to make my hammer and bevel gauges. The school taught these tasks in the first quarter classes, which I would not start until the fall.

I bought a wide plank of fine Honduran mahogany twenty feet long for my toolbox. I built sliding boxes with the whole grain folded around each side and a take-out box for my saws. The instructors were quite impressed. I also made an oar that was a work of art, including the leather strap that protected the wood from the oarlock.

I was in my last six months of boatbuilding school and had already started my personal business, working out of my mother's garage and on boats in the shipyard. I worked on boats in the evenings and weekends and went to school during the day. If I had a problem in the yard, I could take it to the school and say, "What do I do about this?" Between the two, I would have all the help and resources I needed.

CHAPTER FORTY-THREE

Redirecting Energy

*"I realized that every time I thought
I was being rejected from something good,
I was actually being redirected to something better."*

—— **Dr. Steve Maraboli**

THE NORTHWEST SCHOOL of Wooden Boatbuilding is located on Port Townsend Bay, Washington. The public docks are a two-minute walk from the school, and offshore from the public docks are moorings in the bay that people rent. They tie their yachts to the moorings and live on their boats. The boat owners row their dinghies from their live-aboard yachts to the public dock, tie up their dinghies, and then go to work. When they return in the evening, they row their dinghies back to their boats, where they spend the night. What a life, huh? I guess somebody has to do it.

Three young boys lived nearby: Tim, twelve; David, thirteen; and Donny, fourteen. The boys did not have a boat of their own, but they had always wanted one. They loved fishing from the docks where the yacht owners tied up their dinghies. Being young boys, they especially enjoyed engaging in mischief. Irresistibly attracted to the dinghies as a source of entertainment, the boys thought it would be fun to come down to the dock and untie them, leaving them to float away into the bay.

In the words of the immortal Beach Boys, they had 'fun, fun, fun' until they got caught by one of the boat owners. A short 'altercation' ensued, ending with the boat owner throwing the boys into the water of Port Townsend Bay. Unhappy with this 'brutal' treatment of their 'sweet little children,' the boys' parents filed charges against the boat owner. However, when he explained what was happening, it was the boys that got busted instead.

When they appeared in front of the judge at the Port Hadlock Marina, Jim Maupin, the Vice Commodore of the Port Hadlock Yacht Club and a friend of the boat owner, decided to come forward on behalf of the boys and sponsor them. Rather than branding them with a criminal record, Jim Maupin's idea was to let them work off their community service by building their own boat. He convinced the judge of his approach, and now it was a matter of selling the idea to the boys.

The Boatbuilding School had recently moved to its new location on the Port Hadlock waterfront, and they were offering a weeklong boatbuilding class in which the students would construct their own twelve-foot dinghy. In a collaborative effort to get the boys off the street and onto the water, the Port Hadlock Yacht Club, a local United Methodist Church, and the East Jefferson Rotary Club banded together to raise the needed funds to get the boys into the program. Jim Maupin wrote a letter to the boys in care of their parents, asking if they would like to take the class. He also offered to pay for the three boys to take an introductory sailing safety class through the boatbuilding school.

"We were sort of happy because we would get to keep the boat, and we've sort of always wanted one," Tim said about Maupin's letter.

The three spent five eight-hour days assembling the pre-cut pieces for their Skunk Island (flat-bottomed) dinghy. First, they learned where their boat's various parts were. Next, they learned about conditioning their tools and how to use power tools safely.

On the first day, the boys assembled sawhorses to hold the boat and began constructing the frame. They shaped, fitted, and smoothed the rough-cut panels and parts using handsaws and planes.

Despite being the youngest team of three in the program, they stayed ahead of the other two groups as they glued the plywood panels to the frames.

Tim bragged, "We were an hour ahead of everybody else, and we stayed ahead. We were fast."

Jay said, "Let me tell you, friends, these boys were energetic. They very nearly exhausted the instructors. I was so tired at the end of my first day that I didn't bother to eat dinner.

"As the team supervisor, I attributed their speed to the 'hyper energy' the boys brought to the project. Building a boat gave them an outlet for their energy and models of how people interact on the job."

On the second day, the boys got discouraged. They dealt with that by going fishing. But then, came back determined not to take any more breaks.

David said, "If we kept blowing it off, we realized we wouldn't get it done. So, it was work, work, work from then on."

They were willing to redo something even if it was just an eighth of an inch off. Each developed a specialty. One cut out parts, developing expertise with the intimidating band saw that ran continuously, another concentrated on drilling, and the other handled the finish work with the screws.

The boys remarked, "We're learning something we wanted to do, stuff we can use later in life."

After assembling the dinghy, the first time, the boys nearly rebelled at having to tear it down to waterproof it before reassembly.

"It was frustrating," Donny said, "But Jay and Christian, our instructors, told us it would sink otherwise, so we did it all again."

Finally, they started painting and waving the paintbrushes around on the last day. I yelled, "Gloves, gloves, gloves! Now, now, now!" The three didn't give me any grief. Instead, they ran to put on gloves and started the last stage before they could launch the skiff.

"Is it gonna float?" I asked as they painted.

When they launched the boat for its maiden voyage the next day, the boys yelled, "It's floating!" as they started to row away from the shore.

David said, "The boat didn't draw no water, and it held up perfectly."

A proud moment for all. And a victory for these boys.

"It's been pretty amazing to see the transformation in the boys from when they began to when they finished," an administrator from the school said, "Their communication skills, goal setting, listening, hand-eye coordination, and just being able to express themselves have all improved."

I noticed the boys had gained as much as two years of social skills. They had come in with their arms crossed over their chests. In a few days, they had all uncrossed their arms and pushed out their chests. They learned how to interact with adults, ask questions, accept criticism, and that mistakes are not fatal.

They learned to collaborate and work as a team. They came to understand and respect another person's property. And now that they have their own boat, something they sweated on together, how will they feel if someone trespasses on it?

We redirected their energy toward a goal they wanted to achieve. Eventually, they learned how much they could accomplish with teamwork.

That was a lesson for life that they will never forget. I was honored to be a part of that. I wish someone had redirected my energy in a more productive way when I was younger.

Ever since high school, I had been doing bad things. So, when I got to the boat school, it was an opportunity for me to start doing good things, and it was the happiest time of my life. I was free. I was able to do things. I was exploring myself and learning new details about myself and my desires. The instructors I had were some of the finest men of character and skill you could ever hope to work for. And the palette for the expression of their art was a wooden boat.

I graduated from the Northwest School of Wooden Boatbuilding in 2005 with an Associate of Occupational Studies degree in Contemporary Wood Composites, specializing in composite (cold-molded) construction techniques and interior joinery.

It was the time of my life. Finally, I had accomplished something significant and good and built a foundation for a legitimate, honest business and career.

Surprisingly, however, within a week or two after graduation, my mother came to me and said, "You gotta leave. You gotta get out of the house. Go. Goodbye. Go back to Texas."

For the life of me, I don't understand why, and she offered no explanation.

Maybe she was just being the 'mama bird' kicking the baby bird out of her nest.

CHAPTER FORTY-FOUR

When the Dove Sings

"Therefore, if anyone is in Christ,
he is a new creation;
the old has gone, the new has come!"

—— **2 Corinthians 5:17 (NIV)**

PJ AND I MOVED back to Texas in 2005 and settled in a little town called Gordonville, an unincorporated community of less than fifteen hundred near Lake Texoma. The Texas-Oklahoma border follows the Red River through the middle of the lake.

We had been in Gordonville for about three months. I had no job. I had talked to everybody, but when they saw that I was a convicted felon, they didn't want to deal with me. Not even Walmart would hire me as a greeter, where all I would have to say is, "Welcome to Walmart! Now, get your shit and get out!" I could do that. I'm sure I could do that.

The Bible calls for the husband to be the spiritual leader of the home. However, in the case of our house, PJ was clearly the leader. Although I was trying to catch up, she was far ahead of me in her spiritual walk.

We were staying at the apartment of a friend of PJ's. When PJ went to work, I would take the canoe to Treasure Island on Lake Texoma with my Bible and just sit out there and read. I was trying to learn. PJ gave me a book on Luke, which was an eye-opening experience. It provided a narrative explanation for every topic, which really helped my understanding.

In the *Gospel of Matthew*, the stated mission of John the Baptist was to "Prepare the way for the Lord and make straight the paths for [Jesus Christ]" (Matthew 3:3 NIV). He explained his approach to accomplishing this by saying, "I baptize you with water for repentance. But after me will come one who is more powerful than I, whose sandals I am not fit to carry. He will baptize you with the Holy Spirit and with fire" (Matthew 3:11 NIV).

The *Book of Acts* describes the realization of this prophecy, saying, "When the day of Pentecost came, [the Apostles] were all together in one place. Suddenly, a sound like the blowing of a violent wind came from Heaven and filled the whole house where they were sitting. They saw what seemed to be tongues of fire that separated and came to rest on each of them. All of them were filled with the Holy Spirit and began to speak in other tongues as the Spirit enabled them." (Acts 2:1-4 NIV)

Even though I wanted Christ in my life, my true conversion was a real process.

I believe that my definitive path to redemption and salvation began in 2000, with me calling out to God for help in the depths of my despair while suffering my time in the Hole at FCI Seagoville. A year later, after I returned home from prison, I began attending church services at the Central Baptist Church in Sulphur Springs but for all the wrong reasons, specifically concerning what others thought of me by using the church as a banner of 'I am good enough.'

After listening to the Word of God in that church for about four months, I made my profession of faith, verbally giving myself over to God. Two weeks later, the Pastor baptized me with water, witnessed by my mother.

In the eyes of the church, I was saved. But the real change was yet to come.

<<<>>>

In 2008, PJ and I moved to Pottsboro, Texas, a similarly sized town about twenty-five miles east of Gordonville near Lake Texoma. There, we attended the Lakeway United Methodist Church. PJ had joined a group called Walk to Emmaus [7] and went through the entire program, even becoming a lay director for one of the walks in Dallas years before we even met.

"I want you to go to a *Walk to Emmaus* retreat for a couple of days," PJ told me. "Dan and Pat Farrarr from the church will sponsor you." Pat was my Sunday School teacher at the time.

I said, "Okay. Sure. I'll do it." Of course, I had no understanding of the nature of this commitment, but I went anyway, and it turned out to be the most pivotal moment of my entire spiritual walk.

The *Walk to Emmaus* is a structured program sponsored by Upper Room Ministries. Its stated purpose is to "develop Christian disciples and leaders by equipping active adult church members for Christian action."

The Body of Christ was revealed to me in the most profound way on one special night during the program. It was a majestic love that blew me away.

When it happened, my legs were shaking, and I was crying. It changed me in the most magical way. Like the tongues of fire of the Holy Spirit that came to rest on the Apostles on the day of Pentecost, *this moment was my baptism by the Holy Spirit.*

It was like a veil had lifted off my eyes, and I could see everything clearly. The trees were vibrating, the colors of the sky were dynamic, and everything was fresh and new. *I could feel the energy coming off me, and I knew from that moment that God had changed my heart. And it was then that He had made me a new creation.*

After that, God's Word jumped out at me whenever I opened the Bible. Words between the words, lines between the lines. Impressions. God's Word was calling out to me. He had turned the key, and revelation built upon revelation, faith upon faith.

In my reading, I learned that, in Christianity, a dove symbolizes the Holy Spirit, along with new beginnings, peace, fidelity, love, and prosperity. I remembered my mother and I attending the Methodist revival meeting in Longview forty-eight years earlier in 1960. The pastor had talked about this in his prayer. Then I realized what he meant by, "When the Dove sings."

Powerful, powerful. It took my breath away. I had the absolute sense that the old man in me had died that day, and the new man in me had been born.

That was the pivotal moment of my salvation. That was the moment of my being spiritually reborn. And that was when I indeed became a member of the Body of Christ.

"When the Dove sings*," I whispered. Yes! I get it now. This is the baptism by the Holy Spirit!*

I am baptized by the Holy Spirit. Praise the Lord!

It has been an incredible walk since then – blessings upon blessings. I think about when I was in the belly of the beast, dead for years. Then I was reborn, back into society. Finally, I was reborn into the Body of Christ. Praise God!

After that, I attended the *Walk to Emmaus* every year for ten years. And I can definitely see the effect on my behavior as an individual. I had not been running on all eight cylinders. But each time I attended, I came back, and it was like, here I am again, back in the lap of God's love, grace, and blessings.

I received training through the Methodist church to become a certified lay speaker, allowing me to conduct worship services, preach, and lead Bible studies as requested by the pastor. It would also allow me to have my own church under the supervision of a pastor in Oklahoma.

However, I did not really feel ready to have my own church. So, I continued my education toward the certification, but I didn't know if He wanted me to have a church or if He wanted me just to go out and be a witness.

I suppose I may have a church someday, but realistically speaking, I would need to be retired to have one. At this point, I cannot retire. I spent all my money when I was younger; now I will have to work until the day I die. Because I was a convicted felon, I could not get employment. I could only be self-employed. Consequently, I have no retirement savings and no social security. I have nothing. This frustrates the hell out of PJ because a woman wants the security that she will be provided for if her man dies. I have insurance on each of us such that if we were to die, it would pay off our debts automatically. That provides some degree of security. Not the best, but it's something.

In an attempt to expand my prison ministry, I visited the kids at the Collin County Detention Center in McKinney, Texas, on several occasions, and their program was a real eye-opener. I wanted to replicate that program at the Grayson County Juvenile Detention Center in Sherman, Texas. They heard my story but did not want to let me in. "What can you contribute to these kids?" they asked.

"I can give them hope," I answered.

It rang a bell with them, but they never called me back. Various ministers from there have tried to get me in to talk to the juvenile inmates, but they won't allow me.

Prison ministry is very important to me, but I don't know what will happen. I have a story that I need to tell, and I can tell it. I have said it to many people in the *Walk to Emmaus* program. I have a presentation to follow for what the program is trying to promote. Still, at the prisons, I'm allowed only three minutes to interject my personal experience related to the program. I have more to say than that.

Jonah was a prophet whom God called to preach in the foreign city of Nineveh. Instead, Jonah tried to escape God, but a great fish swallowed him.

When the fish returned him to land, Jonah went to Nineveh and warned the people about God's judgment. Jonah learned, to his dismay, that God would forgive even a heathen city if the people confessed their sins and repented.

When it comes to my criminal life, I have difficulty talking about myself because I once was a proud, arrogant, pompous ass, and I never want to be that again. I want to be invisible, but I know that God is asking me to do something, and I have to get up in front of people to do it. He has been chasing me for a long time now. So, I know what He wants me to do. But I'm like Jonah. God is calling me to do something for Him, but I don't want to do it, and I am well experienced at running away.

However, we need to realize that it wasn't the three days Jonah spent in the belly of the great fish that had the momentous effect; it was what he did afterward in Nineveh. And so, in my situation, what

I went through is not so important, but what I can do with it afterward is.

I want to glorify God, but I am afraid that I will have to publicly confess ugly things about myself, which I am not proud of, and I am very uncomfortable with that.

But I know I must ultimately do His will at some point if He is to be glorified. And so, I am sure I shall.

Amen, and amen.

CHAPTER FORTY-FIVE

The Confession

*"If we confess our sins,
He is faithful and just
and will forgive us our sins
and purify us from all unrighteousness."*

— 1 JOHN 1:9 (NIV)

AFTER COMPLETING MY TRAINING through the Methodist church to become a certified lay speaker, Pastor Dan McMillen of the San Juan Baptist Church invited me to speak to his congregation on the topic "Can Any Good Come from a Bad Choice?" He wanted me to speak about some things that happened in my life. Other than Pastor McMillen and my wife, no one in that church knew about these things. Not even my Bible study family, to whom I felt as close as anyone in that church, knew about this.

So, this is the big secret I told them on that Sunday Morning.

"First, I will confess to you that I have made many bad choices. I will tell you that the consequences of those choices were quite significant. Unfortunately, these actions affected not only me but also my family – my mother, sister, and brothers, as well as my friends. But the good news is that those bad choices eventually led me to reconcile with my Heavenly Father and to call on Jesus Christ to be my Lord and Savior. And I believe this likely added many years to my life on Earth.

"So, yes, my bad choices ultimately did bring good into my life in the long run. But it was only after I understood my Father's love

245

and grace, which would become evident as the result of my bad choices.

"I am reminded of the Bible story of the potter, the potter's wheel, and the mound of clay on his wheel. The potter molded the clay into shape with the pressure exerted by his hands on this previously formless lump, creating a vessel designed for the shape and purpose of the potter's will.

"Similarly, the pressure of God's hands shaped and molded me through the consequences of my bad choices. The good that came from those bad choices was the realization of the possibility for honor, integrity, courage, perseverance, strength, clarity of purpose, and dedication. But, most of all, the good that manifested from my bad choices was understanding the blessings of walking each day with my Father and holding His hand tightly.

"Prior to that, I was operating under the illusion that through these bad choices I made in my past, I would be running and playing among the joys of this 'world,' but this would soon pale in comparison to the joy of coming face-to-face with my Savior, which literally took me to my knees, trembling in awe.

"My past actions were only my attempt to escape into a state of 'feeling good in the moment.' Unfortunately, they ultimately would leave me empty in heart and soul when the sun rose the next morning.

"I am here today to tell you that the good that came from the bad choices of my past is the realization of God's love and grace, which none of us deserve, and of the clean slate we enjoy each morning simply because He calls us His own. But, of course, the most significant benefit is that He has written my name with own His hand in the Book of Life.

"It is a fact that even though we have all made some bad choices in our lives and may still be encountering harsh consequences for those decisions, God always has a way of recasting them for good if we are just willing to turn to Him and trust Him with our future.

"A dear friend of mine who knew of the talk I would give this morning pointed me to a favorite scripture she thought would be applicable.

"Hebrews 8:12 says, 'For I will be merciful and gracious toward their sins, and I will remember their deeds of unrighteousness no more.'

"Many people with whom I have spoken about my faith believe their walk with Christ is heavy and a burden that requires them to change things they don't want to change. But I remind them of the words of the Apostle Matthew, 'For my yoke is easy, and my burden is light.'" (Matthew 11:30 NIV)

"So, what were those bad choices from my past where good has come into my life?"

[Long, quiet pause.]

"I was a three times convicted drug felon, viewed by the law as a career criminal."

[Another pause.]

"I was sentenced to twenty-five years in a federal penitentiary for smuggling marijuana from Mexico and South America across the Texas border into our homeland for almost twenty years."

[Long pause, and then tearfully.]

"This is not something I am proud of.

"But I am thankful for God's grace, His love that continually manifests itself in my life, and the revelation of Himself to me through these bad choices."

[Another pause with head dropped humbly.]

"Knowing all this, I hope you can find me worthy to be accepted as a sinner into your holy community.

Thank you. God bless you all.

Amen, and Amen."

CHAPTER FORTY-SIX

The Limit of Desperation

"Oh, my God, Jerry!
What have you done?"

—— **Jerry Kitchens' Realtor**

JERRY KITCHENS CONTINUED to threaten us quite often. When we moved back to Texas, there were times when we felt like someone had been in our house during the night watching us.

Three years later, we got a call from a friend who told us that Jerry had some health issues. Having no more information than that, we just assumed it may have been cancer. Jerry lived in Quitman, where he cared for his mother, who had advanced Alzheimer's disease.

One day soon after that, Jerry called a local real estate agent to put his house on the market. "Would you please come over here to discuss selling my house?" he asked.

When the very willing realtor arrived, anxious and excited at the prospect of getting a new listing, she opened the gate and drove in, only to find Jerry lying in the driveway.

"Oh, my God, Jerry! What have you done?" she cried.

Once the realtor calmed down a bit, she went into the house and called the police.

Since there were no witnesses and no suicide note, the rumor mill had a field day trying to figure out what happened. We were all under the impression that Jerry may have received some terrible news about his cancer diagnosis. Maybe he just didn't want to have

249

to endure chemotherapy. Perhaps he was one of those people who preferred quality over quantity. Or maybe, he still wanted to punish PJ and me for betraying him and make us feel guilty about that. I don't know. No one knows. Instead, Jerry had called the appropriate people and handled his affairs before the end.

Left with nothing but conjecture, it was generally regarded and tentatively confirmed by the Wood County Medical Examiner that after he called the realtor, Jerry walked half-way to the front gate, leaving his mother inside the house. He then put the muzzle of a short-barrel twelve-gauge shotgun into his mouth and literally blew his head off.

When the police arrived, they found Jerry Kitchens' Alzheimer's-ridden mother alone in the house, unharmed and oblivious to the death of her only son.

CHAPTER FORTY-SEVEN

Emerson Bay Boatworks

*"The mission of Emerson Bay Boatworks
is to preserve, restore, repair, and protect
these precious examples of days gone by."*

—— **Jay Emerson**

PJ AND I MOVED TO POTTSBORO, Texas, in 2008, and I opened a four-thousand-square-foot shop at Grandpappy Point Marina on the Red River at Lake Texoma. Thus, was born Emerson Bay Boatworks, a full-service shop for the restoration of antique and classic wooden boats. A sign over the door read:

Emerson Bay Boatworks

"Where the Journey Begins"

Over the last fifteen years, I developed a solid business built almost entirely through personal relationships and word-of-mouth referrals. I have done restoration and repair work, specializing in antique and classic boats. I've done boats of sizes ranging from canoes to runabouts to cruisers to yachts. These vessels are predominately made from mahogany and white oak and may be powered by inboard engines. I've done major brands like Chris-Crafts, Gar Woods, Hacker Crafts, Centuries, Shepherds, Owens, and a rare Carter. My own personal boat I was in the process of restoring was a 1932 Richardson 30-foot Launch. She was extraordinary.

All antique and classic boats are magnificently beautiful, not just aesthetically, but also because of their character as demonstrated by the cuts and bruises earned over a lifetime of service. These boats are historic treasures to be admired, respected, preserved, and meticulously cared for. The mission of Emerson Bay Boatworks is to preserve, restore, repair, and protect these precious examples of days gone by.

Generally speaking, since being in this business, I have never wanted for work. Right now, I have four boats on site and a backlog of work stretching a year out. I have my winter projects lined up. Yet I am trying to slow this thing down. I'm a seventy-one year-old senior citizen now, a fact of which my body is painfully aware. Sometimes, I think, physically, I may have only one more year of this kind of work in me. But thanks to my backlog of work and the relationships I have built over the years, I feel I have a little job security, enough to make me feel reasonably confident and secure for at least the next year.

Emerson Bay Boatworks is the ultimate manifestation of my dream that originated with the loan of a copy of *Woodenboat* magazine back in FCI Texarkana a long, long time ago. Thank you, Lord. This is the new creation I have become.

CHAPTER FORTY-EIGHT

The General Lee

"Jesus knows the burdens we carry
and the tears we shed,
but He is the healer of broken hearts,
broken dreams, and broken lives.
Trust him. He never fails."

—— **John Hagee**

AN EMERSON BAY BOATWORKS customer named Lee Varnidore invited me to the Lake of the Ozarks in central Missouri in 2009 to advise him on a boat restoration he was doing. While touring the marina, I discovered a 1932 Richardson 30-foot Launch, known then as *Yahooz*. Fortunately, the boat happened to be for sale. For me, it was love at first sight – her wood, her sheer line, the way she sat in the water, and the pilot's station reminiscent of the *African Queen*. She was plain pretty, and I had to have her.

Eleven months later, we finally completed the process of buying and transporting the boat to Lake Texoma. I arranged to have the Richardson towed across the lake to a marina where we could load her onto a transport vehicle with the help of a travel lift.

The Richardson had been neglected for almost three years when I found her at the slip. While she was under tow, I became concerned about the water bubbling up from the exposed seams in the hull bottom. But soon the bilge pumps kicked in and kept her afloat. Nevertheless, I kept running from the steering station to the cabin below to ensure everything was going according to plan. I knew the boat had to have a heart and a soul. After being tied to a slip for all those years, getting back into the open water seemed to give her a sense of the new life awaiting her just around the bend.

After the thirty-minute tow across the lake, the travel lift was in sight, and the real chore of getting her onto the transport vehicle had finally come. The boat was seventy-eight years old, and I had heard horror stories about boats getting on the travel lift. Sometimes, they fell apart in mid-section due to an error in supporting the vessel under the frames, or the boat might be so rotten that the weight worked against the lift, and the collapsed hull came crashing down.

Once we secured her on the trailer, we all could relax a bit, but we weren't done yet. We still had to be sure she could safely make the long ride home to Texas. Once the trip to Texas was complete, we could start on the next step – unloading her onto the pad next to my house in Pottsboro, where her restoration process would begin.

However, with only one more corner to make before we backed her up into the pad, the truck needed to make a very wide turn into a vacant lot to make the corner, and, of course, it got stuck. Thankfully, the boom truck came to the rescue and pulled the Richardson to freedom.

Finally, arriving safely on the home front, we set the Richardson in place for her restoration. First, we shored up the stern on jack stands and then used the boom truck to lift the front end of the boat so we could pull the trailer out from under her. After the trailer was free and the boat suspended with the boom truck, we strategically placed jack stands to keep the Richardson steady and put blocks under the keel to keep her straight and level.

My team, consisting of employees, friends, and neighbors, started with documentation and measurements, taking photos at every step in the restoration process. Then, as we removed each part, the team tagged them and made extensive notes of their positions and conditions. Next, we removed the transom to allow the bilge to dry and to clean out all the years of muck that had accumulated. After that, we examined for rot every part of the skeleton sections of the boat, including the keel, stem, backbone, and frames.

In 2011, I moved the Richardson to a position on the lower level of my Emerson Bay Boatworks shop at Grandpappy Point Resort and Marina on Lake Texoma, where the restoration work would continue as time permitted, considering that my customers' boats would come first. After that, I began referring to the boat as the *General Lee*, after my retired Marine friend Lee Varnidore.

Life was good, it seemed.

And then came the flood.

After suffering through four consecutive years of extreme drought, many Texas lakes closed to boating due to extraordinarily low water levels. Then, the summer of 2015 brought record levels of rainfall to Texas. By mid-July, the water level at Lake Texoma crested at almost six hundred forty-six feet, more than twenty-nine feet above normal levels. Now more than five and a half feet over its spillway, the lake released approximately one hundred thousand cubic feet per second of water, while at the same time, even more water than that was flowing into the lake from rain, and upstream lakes and rivers.

The flooding catastrophically affected my shop, which was located at the water's edge. As the rising water level approached the shop doors, I made an urgent plea to my friends and family to help me save my customers' boats, along with my tools and equipment. People stepped up with trailers. They stepped up with their own bodies. If they couldn't come with their bodies, they sent their children to help me.

Leaving my own boat for last, I could not get the *General Lee* out since it would have taken an eighteen-wheeler to do so, and there was simply not enough time for that, considering the levels already reached by the floodwaters and rising by the hour.

The best we could do for the *General Lee* was to prepare her to weather the storm as well as we could. My helpers and I pulled the engine, reamed the caulk between the hull bottom planks, and drilled three holes in the garboard planks, which were the rows of planks on either side of the keel, at the bow for drainage. We secured the hull with jack stands and supported it with wooden blocks. The fate of the *General Lee* was now out of the hands of men.

In a matter of only days, the water rose to a level eight feet above the upper floor of the shop. Positioned by herself on the lower floor, which comprised a ramp that sloped down into the lake, the rising waters quickly overtook the *General Lee.* When the water had reached her top decks and the highest point of the pilot's station was a mere four feet from the shop's ceiling, the Richardson floated off her stands and listed sharply to the starboard side. It appeared that the *General Lee* would imminently be lost to the flood and possibly destroyed.

With the boat now floating on its own, using a Jon boat with a nine-horsepower outboard engine, I pushed and tugged the *General Lee* out the bay door of the lower floor of the shop, around the building, and back in through the bay door of the upper floor where I moored her to the wall. The boat settled to the floor on its keel when the water receded. Then, having no electricity in the shop because of the flooding, I used a compressor to inflate airbags to lift the boat enough to allow me to get jack stands back under it.

Thinking the boat now safe proved presumptuous when a second flood came in a few days, and the water rose to within six inches of its previous height. The *General Lee* once again floated off its stands, but this time, it came down hard on them when the water finally receded, leaving a few new repairs to consider, but safe and generally sound.

The flood was a crushing blow to me, both economically and emotionally, forcing me to rethink my need and desire for such a large shop. Deciding a more personal, one-on-one approach might better serve my craft, I chose not to return to the shop at Grandpappy Point Resort and Marina.

I moved my shop back to my home in Pottsboro, where I focused my efforts on smaller runabouts, those from eighteen to thirty feet in length. The *General Lee* remained at the shop at Grandpappy's.

In 2016, PJ and I moved to McAlester, Oklahoma, her hometown, to be nearer to her family and her roots. I established a new shop at our house and continued my business, convincing my customers to make the hundred-mile trip from Dallas for service. Thankfully, most were willing to come.

After our move to McAlester, the Richardson remained in the shop at Grandpappy's for quite some time. In the meantime, thieves removed all the copper hardware and the nose block, which was the hand-carved bulb-shape nose on the bow. Losing the nose block caused a hogged keel, meaning the keel was no longer straight but slightly bowed, which would negatively affect the performance of the boat if not repaired. By then, there was no point in bringing her home to restore. She was a total loss. Eventually, the marina cut up and burned the *General Lee*.

Sad, very sad. These boats are to be saved, not lost. These classic wooden boats are magnificent, beautiful works of art. They are relics from yesteryear when the world was quite different from the one we know today. In addition to beauty, they are unique and have heritage, character, and historical value. Properly restored classic boats are quite valuable.

Now that I am seventy-one years old and the Richardson is gone, so is my dream of building a boat to sail around the world. It's sad, but that's what happens in life. If never fulfilled, our dreams evaporate, and we are left with only our memories of them. But it makes for a pleasant memory. And you know what happens when you quit dreaming – you die. So, we are left with finding a new dream.

CHAPTER FORTY-NINE

A Day of Reckoning

"A Day of Reckoning –
A day when the consequences
of a course of mistakes or misdeeds are felt."

—— Merriam-Webster Dictionary

ONE CAN PROCLAIM themselves legitimate, but it is real only if others can observe it. My original sentence for the Memphis Operation called for two hundred ninety-two months confinement, followed by ten years of supervised release and a twenty-five-thousand-dollar fine.

The government released me from the Federal Correctional Institution Seagoville on May 11, 2001. However, I still faced ten years of probation. So, in April 2005, I campaigned to have my probationary period reduced. I solicited character reference letters from some of the key members of my new life, and they provided some beautiful words supporting my efforts. The following are excerpts from some of them.

With God's help, Jay is striving to make positive, life-enriching choices to be as productive as possible in advancing positive values back into the lives of others.

I believe Jay to be a fine man who genuinely contributes positively to the life of our church and community. His fine qualities include being a hard worker, having an affirming spirit, a very outgoing disposition, and a readiness and willingness to help.

—— Dan McMillen
Pastor, San Juan Baptist Church

The Schooner Martha Foundation operates a sail training program on board the historic eighty-four-foot schooner Martha. Jay was a tremendous volunteer with our organization for over a year. Not only did he always show up and work hard, but he came with a joyous attitude and work ethic. In addition, Jay has continued to help our foundation by volunteering to write a grant proposal for future funding for our restoration project.

—— Robert D'Arcy
Captain, *Martha*

We are rebuilding an older boat, and Jay has been working with us doing boat cabinetry for almost a year while attending the Northwest School of Wooden Boatbuilding.

He is a hard worker, and we trust him implicitly. He takes full responsibility for his assignments and always does an excellent job with great attention to detail and pride in the beauty of his accomplishments.

—— Donald Dunhaupt
and Mandy Hackney

Last summer, Jay Emerson volunteered to be the assistant instructor for the family boatbuilding workshop, which provides a boatbuilding opportunity for the community's at-risk youth. He was in charge of training this group.

He has an exceptional talent for working with youth. He quickly countered whenever the students demonstrated negative attitudes by redirecting their actions down a positive, productive path. For these students, it was the first time they had completed such an enormous task, and that success significantly impacted their self-esteem. The success and future of that program are primarily due to Jay Emerson.

—— Patti Walden
Northwest School of Wooden Boatbuilding

Jay has been a student in the Interior Joinery course at the Northwest School of Wooden Boatbuilding for the last year. He has been an outstanding and energetic presence in the classroom and on the shop floor. Additionally, to add to his experience at school, he has found work in the trade in the evenings and on weekends.

While volunteering to work with at-risk youth in our Family Boatbuilding summer program, Jay took three troubled teenagers under his wing, and together they constructed a small rowing skiff. After watching the relationship between Jay and the boys develop over the week, I'm sure this was a positive and quite possibly pivotal experience in their lives due to Jay's genuine enthusiasm and 'can do' attitude.

—— **Jeff Hammond**
Northwest School of Wooden Boatbuilding

Steven Gregoryk was my U.S. Probation Officer in Everett, Washington. At my request, he scheduled my hearing on the matter for April 2005.

Nevertheless, despite all the lovely words and thoughts expressed in the letters, I served my time, or twelve years of it anyway. I did every day of the entire ten-year probation term and paid the twenty-five-thousand-dollar fine.

Just as my father once told me, eventually, there comes *a day of reckoning*.

And that's a good thing, as I have learned.

More importantly, those letters represented love, appreciation, and respect. They suggested that I may have finally achieved the legitimacy in my life for which I have strived, at least in their eyes. And that's something.

Praise God!

CHAPTER FIFTY

The Ripples from Our Stones

"Why should any living man
complain when punished for his sins?"

—— **Lamentations 3:39 (NIV)**

IT WAS NOT THE MARIJUANA that eventually got me incarcerated. It was the smuggling, the greed, the power, and the arrogance, along with the attitude of, "I'm going to do my thing, and the hell with what everybody else thinks."

But did society really intend to put human beings through the degrading and dehumanizing aspects of prison? If an inmate was not a criminal before being admitted into the system, then he will become one before his time of incarceration within that house of horrors is over.

Incarceration does not discriminate. It tolerates everyone and anyone. There is not much reason to exclude somebody when they are already excluded from everything else by being sent here.

Since I have been locked up, I have separated my "self" from the person physically having this experience. And I have been trying to be an observer only. So, with these observations, I would like to try to convey some of the truths, as I have seen them, that the judicial system of American prisons is not the solution that man is seeking to rehabilitate the criminal mind.

I have learned that the isolation within the walls of prison can be more tolerable if you can think of yourself as a *'contemplative penitent'* instead of an *'incarcerated felon.'*

Let's consider the meaning of the term 'contemplative penitent,' as defined in the Miriam-Webster Dictionary. First, 'contemplative' is an adjective meaning, "Given to concentration on spiritual things as a form of private devotion." It can also be a noun, meaning, "A person who practices contemplation." Second, 'penitent' is an adjective meaning, "Feeling or expressing humble or regretful pain or sorrow for sins or offenses." It can also be a noun, meaning, "A person who repents of sin."

As for myself, I see the illusion of prison because of the Yogic training I have practiced over the years. I stay centered with breathing exercises dealing with the life-force energies around us and with my mind's eye focused on the inner strength in my heart. I am one of the lucky ones who will not be permanently scarred from the experiences of incarceration within those walls. While it is true that I do have scars, as we all do, I choose to not let them dictate the rest of my life.

From the Bureau of Prisons' foresight, there is definite comfort in the daily routine. Someone can feel a great deal of comfort from 'codified monotony.' Systematic repetition of familiar tasks is the best and safest narcotic.

One of the lessons that God has taught me from this path I have taken in life is that one of life's challenges is to use the power of love to turn disaster into glory. I have accomplished this by remembering that everything happening cannot affect the real 'me.' The forces of life are in constant flux, so I feel that I have to flow with the different aspects of my nature within this experience. I must change, as it were, the real me who is experiencing these times to grow with them and to develop into the whole person that is to be. I have weathered the seasonal changes of my soul in there and become a more genuine person with my 'self' and others. There is truth to the saying, 'the misfortune you experience never lasts a lifetime.'

Life itself is a race marked with a start and a finish. What we learn during the race and how we apply it determines whether our participation has value. If we learn from each success and each failure and improve ourselves through this process, we will have fulfilled our potential and performed well.

There is a lot of faith in prison. Not much else, it's true, but that we do have. It doesn't take up much space, and the government can't take it away from us, and every man watches over his store of faith. It's not only valuable for a place like this, but it's also damn necessary. Otherwise, you despair, and in despairing, you lose your soul. The government can take away your freedom but not your soul. We are less than free, yet we are more than dead. Faith keeps us from dying.

In retrospect, I can see that the destructive impact of marijuana extended to cover even my own personal life's dreams.

As a younger man, I had the ambition and desire to be an Oceanographer/Marine Biologist. I wanted to go to the La Jolla Oceanographic Institute for school. I had grown up on the ocean, swimming and snorkeling in the Pacific Ocean, and every week, I watched Jacques Cousteau and his documentaries aboard the *Calypso*.

Pursuing such an honorable profession as Oceanography would have been noble because I would be trying to understand the world around us and how we can cohabitate and protect it. Those are essential values for stewards of God's creation.

Unfortunately, because of my own life choices, that beautiful opportunity was never to be. But frankly, I don't think of it often these days. It is simply a thing of the past. On the other hand, it is one of those unfulfilled dreams that have a cumulative effect on us over the years.

For a time after I got out of prison, I was still trying to figure out my role in society. Then, finally, collectors on the Northeast Coast bought some of my model boats, and I sold some online.

Eventually, I realized that money is not the best thing in the world. It's nice to have, and it pays the rent, but when you set money as the focal point of your life, I think you lose sight of really living. So, I've always had a spiritual nature about things, and I believe things happen for a reason and always for the good of God.

The things I have gone through have made me who I am today and taught me to be happy and content with who I am. In 1970, when all my criminal activities started, I was seventeen – young and invincible. I am seventy-one now – an old man. There will be no more risky business and no more looking over my shoulder. If I were living in a cardboard box right now, I would be happy because I am mentally, spiritually, and physically free.

Even with as much manipulation and coercion as Buck Cameron applied to me to participate in his criminal schemes, I do not blame him for my outcomes. He was simply an avenue through which I could conduct my own power struggle.

My self-esteem was so low in high school that I used these opportunities with Buck to gain attention to help achieve my dream of becoming a 'kingpin.' I remember the day I went to see Buck at his daddy's house when I was a senior in high school. I told Buck, "Hey, we've been doing a couple of lids here and there, so I'd like to get with you because I know you've got some sources."

"No, I don't want to do that," he said, "You don't need to be doing that. That is not what you're supposed to do."

So, I said, "If you don't give it to me, I'll go somewhere else. So, either you give it to me and profit from it, or I'll go to someone else and get it."

I have to take full responsibility for my choices. The problem was that once I aligned with Buck as his lieutenant, he used this position to manipulate me to do things that no one else would do.

However, these are choices that when it comes right down to it, and when I'm standing there facing Jesus Christ on Judgment Day, there will be no one more responsible than me. And this is the bottom line of it all.

CHAPTER FIFTY-ONE

Epilogue

"Even though I was once a blasphemer,
and a persecutor, and a violent man,
I was shown mercy because I acted in ignorance and unbelief.
The grace of our Lord was poured out on me abundantly,
along with the faith and love that are in Christ Jesus."

—— 1 Timothy 1:13, 14 (NIV)

I AM JAY CALDWELL EMERSON, formerly known only as inmate 11699-077, a three-time convicted felon – a career criminal – once sentenced to twenty-five years in a federal prison for drug-related charges.

Most of the events in this story happened in the last half of the Twentieth Century. In the ensuing years, my memory diminished a fair amount, due to the simple passage of time, the normal aging process, a variety of medical issues, and the massive quantities of drugs I consumed over the years. Nevertheless, I endeavored to tell this story as accurately and thoroughly as possible. But it was not the facts regarding the events, dates, places, or people involved that matter. Instead, it was essential to convey the story of the transformation of my heart, soul, and mind.

I desperately wanted to run away from having to tell this story because doing so was extraordinarily difficult and painful. The simple recollection of the memories was a substantial emotional struggle. The public confession of my sins was even more painful, and it shamed me to my core. But I knew in my heart that I must confess the truth if I were ever to achieve the redemption I so desperately sought.

I fervently hope this book might reach someone in need and touch their heart and mind. Perhaps a hardened criminal facing a long prison sentence as was I. Or a young person facing troubles and seeing no chance for a productive future for themselves. Or someone in the grasp of alcohol or drugs. Or perhaps an everyday person facing a divorce or the loss of a loved one. I pray that my story will show them that the possibility exists to experience a favorable outcome in their lives.

The solution is simple and within your reach. Just call on the Lord God, and He will lift you up, dust you off, and take the pain from your heart. Then He will tenderly kiss you on the forehead and hug you tightly until you think you can't breathe. And He will never let you go, but you will breathe, live, and live like you never believed possible. And you will thank Him endlessly and praise His Holy name.

—— **Jay Caldwell Emerson**
Your Brother in Christ

Attributions

Act One – Criminal Aspirations
[1] **Cannabis Leaf**
What are cannabis leaves? | Cannabis Glossary | Leafly.
https://www.leafly.com/learn/cannabis-glossary/leaf

Chapter Seven – A Normally Dysfunctional Family
[2] **PTSD**
PTSD Treatments – Once A Soldier
https://www.onceasoldier.org/ptsd-treatments/

Chapter Thirteen – Spirit-Filled Hippies
[3] **I Ching**
I Ching | China File
https://www.chinafile.com/keyword/i-ching

Chapter Fifteen – The War on Drugs
[4] **War on Drugs**
History.com Editors: Amanda Onion, Missy Sullivan, Matt
Mullen, and Christian Zapata
Publisher: A&E Television Networks
Original Published Date: May 31, 2017
https://www.history.com/topics/crime/the-war-on-drugs

Chapter Twenty-Nine – Diagnostics
[5] **Diagnostics**
Grant Smaldone, Zoukis Consulting Group
https://federalcriminaldefenseattorney.com/prison-life/prison-security-levels

Chapter Thirty-Three – Messing About In Boats
[6] **The Wind in the Willows**
Playwrite: Kenneth Grahame
Originally Published: October 8, 1908
Publisher: Aladdin; Reprint edition (March 31, 1989)
Illustrators: Ernest H. Shepard (1931), Arthur Rackham (1940), and Charles van Sandwyk (2007)

Chapter Forty-Four – When the Dove Sings
[7] **Walk to Emmaus**
The Upper Room | Walk to Emmaus
https://www.upperroom.org/walktoemmaus

About the Author

Stephen D. Griffitts lives in Mineola, Texas, with his wife, Patrice, and their two boxer dogs, Rowdy and Silk.

Stephen has been writing short stories since 1993 and has a repertoire of over a hundred completed stories, including several writing contest winners.

Since retiring in 2017, Stephen has enjoyed writing books, short stories, and novellas, as well as restoring antique and classic wooden boats. For almost five years, he served as the Managing Editor for *The Brass Bell*, the award-winning quarterly print magazine of the Chris-Craft Antique Boat Club.

In May 2022, Stephen published *In the Shimmering Lights: A Collection of Short Stories and Novellas*. In February 2024, he published *The Ripples from Our Stones: Redeeming Inmate 11699-077*, his first full novel. Both books are available on *Amazon.com* in Kindle and paperback formats.

Stephen is a retired CPA and IT consultant. He spent the finance portion of his career in public accounting and senior financial management roles in various oil and gas companies. For the IT consulting portion of his career, he worked internationally designing and implementing JD Edwards EnterpriseOne software in a variety of clients in Kazakhstan, Angola, Nigeria, Australia, Papua New Guinea, Venezuela, Costa Rica, England, Ireland, Trinidad/Tobago, Canada, and the United States.

Stephen can be reached via e-mail at 48runabout@gmail.com or on *Facebook* under #SDGriffitts1950.

<<<>>>

Jay Caldwell Emerson can be reached via e-mail at jayoklaboats@gmail.com. Jay would enjoy having the opportunity to share his story with your group, church, or ministry.

To learn more about the Walk to Emmaus, visit the Upper Room website at: https://www.upperroom.org/walktoemmaus.

Stephen (left) and Jay (right) at Stephen's wedding to Patrice in September 2016, where Jay served as the Best Man.

Made in the USA
Coppell, TX
07 March 2024

29877640R00164